# THE SELL SMARTER COLLECTION

SCOTT FISHMAN

Copyright © 2016 Scott Fishman All Rights Reserved

# TABLE OF CONTENTS

SHUT UP & LISTEN ............................................................................. 5

FOLLOW YOUR NOES ........................................................................ 13

YOU'VE GOT TO BELIEVE! ................................................................ 21

DON'T BE A LYMAN ........................................................................... 29

SET GOAL-DI-LOCKS ........................................................................ 35

NO PERFECT TIME ............................................................................ 43

DON'T FORGET TO CLOSE ............................................................... 49

I'M JUST BROWSING ........................................................................ 61

"NO" IS JUST THE BEGINNING ........................................................ 67

I'LL QUIT PROCRASTINATING... TOMORROW ................................ 73

ICE CREAM! ....................................................................................... 79

THICKEN YOUR SKIN ........................................................................ 85

AVATARS ARE NOT ALL BLUE ........................................................ 91

ASSUMPTION GUMPTION ................................................................ 99

ALL FOR YOU ................................................................................... 113

YOU HAVE SPOKEN ........................................................................ 115

OBSTACLE COURSE ....................................................................... 117

TEACH & LEARN .............................................................................. 119

| | |
|---|---|
| BE THEIR "GUY" | 123 |
| OUTCOME FOCUSED | 127 |
| THE CONVERSATIONALIST | 129 |
| THINK LIKE AN OWNER | 131 |
| KEEP CALM & GET HEALTHY | 133 |
| CHANGE ON THE FLY | 137 |
| EVERYBODY HURTS...SOMETIMES | 139 |
| PATTERNUS INTERRUPTUS | 143 |
| NO MOBY DICKS | 147 |
| START SMART | 151 |
| SHOW THEM YOU CARE | 153 |
| BE PLEASURABLE | 157 |
| SHOW THEM YOU UNDERSTAND | 159 |
| DON'T BE A SALESMAN | 161 |
| YOU JUST GOT A RAISE | 167 |
| HONE YOUR SCHTICK | 171 |
| READ MORE BOOKS! | 175 |
| THANK YOU | 179 |

# THE 30 MINUTE SALES COACH PRESENTS...

**Sell Smarter**

Seven Simple Strategies For Sales Success

*Dedicated to David Fishman, without whom I would not have this innate power of influence. Watching you gave me the foundation for this exciting and evolving career.*

*Thank you Dad.*

# INTRODUCTION

**"I can't make a sale to save my life."**

We've all heard it before. Even worse, we've all said it before. If it came down to it and you really would die without a sale, you'd find a way to sell.

Standard victim mentality has us immediately blaming the leads, the product, favoritism, nepotism, weather, holidays, etc... It's OK. Like I said, we've all been there.

I am here to give you the secrets to getting past these speed bumps. The truth is, no matter how hard we want to project the fault on external forces, odds are the key to finding sales success lies within you.

I have been there many times in my career. Driving myself nuts trying to figure out why others are finding success while I am getting shot down left and right.

By the same token, I have also been part of the opposite conversation countless times. Fielding calls and emails from peers and leaders asking what I am doing to find success where others are hitting brick walls.

In over two decades in sales, I've learned to recognize when these slumps and streaks are starting in both myself and those around me. Although the problem is not always the same, the root of the problem can be one of many issues that can plague even the best salespeople.

In the pages that follow, we will identify many of these issues and work out solutions to get past them.

**Get out of your own way.**

From the day I started leading and coaching new salespeople, I repeated this mantra: *We are our own worst enemies in so many respects. If we just get past the hurdles we create for ourselves, success is right there.*

Whether we are temporarily insane due to some emotional event, temporary stress, bad sales call, or we rat hole our selves with metrics and all the reasons we cannot succeed, we are 90% of the problem.

It's so easy to see from the outside looking in, but inside that bubble, these obstacles become very real to us. Molehills become mountains. Speed bumps become roadblocks. We create the insurmountable from the minuscule.

Just as any salesperson worth their weight will foreshadow their entire sales process, I believe that making a new salesperson conscious of these common issues up front will make them more cognizant of them when they do occur and they will recognize them either on their own or when they are pointed out by a peer, leader or coach.

In this book, we will examine common obstacles new salespeople put in front of themselves and decode them. We will find ways to not only get around these "roadblocks" but to truly blast right through them.

My goal is to have you recognize these behaviors and emotions in your own day to day and work to squash them. We truly are our own worst enemy at times. Remove that adversary and watch the road to success open up.

It's time to get out of your own way and succeed in sales.

# SHUT UP & LISTEN

**Shut the hell up and listen.**

As salespeople, we are always on stage. Every sales presentation is a performance. Proper preparation means we take time to research our product and also our prospect before we even think of presenting.

The problem is, we often neglect the latter. We overload with product knowledge and skimp on researching our client's needs.

As a result sometimes we come in over-prepared. These cases usually come in when we are at our weakest. I mean, who has time to spend hours over-preparing for a presentation when we are running from appointment to appointment closing sales left and right? Riding a hot streak allows you to fly fast and loose, winning on momentum alone!

It's often when we are slumping that we put so much pressure on ourselves and grip the bat way too tight, trying to make sure we have all bases covered. We forget that the transaction is really just between two humans and over-think it all.

Over-prepping leads to quite a few pitfalls, one of which is such a simple speed bump to get past, yet we fall prey to it over and over. We simply stop listening.

I have seen salespeople from the bottom of production reports to the top fall prey to this. We are the experts after all, so we know what is best for the customer, so we tell them what is best. We put on our little performance and show much we know. The problem is, we know everything there is to know about what we are selling and nothing about who we are selling to.

So if our problem is not truly knowing the client, what is the solution? The answer is pretty darn easy in theory, but surprisingly sometimes very difficult in practice. We just need to shut our mouths and open our ears!

*"Are you really listening... or just waiting for your turn to talk?" – Robert Montgomery*

I have used this line so many times in coaching folks, that at one point, I found myself searching for another quote that embodied the same sentiment in a less sarcastic tone.

*"The quieter you become, the more you can hear." – Ram Dass*

This one not only does the trick, but makes me sound even wiser than I already am.

If you've ever taken a Dale Carnegie course or read one of his books, you know as humans, we have a fondness for talking about ourselves. This is a universal archetype that is rarely deviated from.

Ever go to a family function and get chatted up by a distant Aunt or Uncle that you'd never met and left feeling that you really liked that person? Did you suddenly realize that you actually knew very little about them, but they sure asked a lot of questions about you? The truth is, you fell in like with them because of how they made you feel. You loved telling them all about your crazy summer adventures, sporting events or future plans. I am sure they lived vicariously through you as well, but chances are, you had more fun than they did.

Police and Con Artists alike use this type of social engineering all the time. They get you talking about yourself, and ask you questions leading down a very comfortable path. Before you know it, you are letting out some juicy bit of info that you'd have been better suited keeping to yourself. The next step is changing your passwords or calling an attorney!

We've established that people love talking about themselves, and given the chance will tattle on themselves. Let's use this to our advantage. Think about your last few sales calls. Who did the majority of the talking? If you didn't make the sale, chances are it was you! If so, you're doing it wrong. It's time to shut the fuck up and listen. I mean really listen.

We know that our clients are human. This means it's a pretty sure shot that they will enjoy talking about themselves. Get them talking.

If you're selling to an individual, ask them general questions that you can drill down further into. For instance, if I were selling windows, I might start with "This is a great house you have here. Are you the original owner?" A question like this sometimes gets a quick one word "yes" or "no", but will often open up a whole new line of questioning that can eventually lead into us talking about the windows. We can obtain a ton of info without going right in for the kill and discussing our product such as how old the home is, has it been renovated, how long they plan to stay in the home, budget tolerances, heating/cooling costs, style preferences, etc… All of this info can be found before we offer up any info about our product.

Now our sales pitch can be molded on the fly to help address their specific needs without sounding like a canned presentation.

What sounds better?

Holding up a sample window: "Our patented three-ply glass coating has special polymers that will dramatically reduce your heating and cooling costs each year."

or

Handing them the sample window: "You mentioned this place was a bitch to keep cool in the summer. Check this out. Our windows have this space age coating, kind of like your iPhone screen. It keeps hot on the hot side and cold on the cold side. Feel how cool this stays? This will get that AC bill down for sure."

Not only are you offering them a benefit vs. a feature, but you are also relating it directly to them based on a concern you uncovered while listening to them early on. You are able to touch the emotional nerve vs. just giving them facts. People buy on emotion. They justify with logic.

Had you just walked in and started out with "Tell me why you want new windows", the answer is more often than not that the old ones are just old, or they are ugly and don't match. By having the initial fact finding conversation casually, people will tell you the real reason they want to buy and not just the answer they think you are looking for.

Note the word casual above. Nothing reeks of evidence collection more than a guy with a clipboard. Captain Clipboard will always put people on edge. Taking notes is fine, but do it casually. If I am the window guy, I have a small notepad that I keep in my pocket and take notes sparingly so I am armed with the proper ammo later. Remember, our goal is to get them talking, not to have a game of verbal Ping-Pong ensue.

What happens when you get that client who is just such a defensive nerd that he/she won't give up any info? We've all had these customers. They play their cards so close to the vest in fear that they will give you that one nugget of info that allows you to go for the jugular and leave them penniless wearing nothing but an old barrel.

First off, you are smart enough to buy this book and I assume good enough to have closed at least one sale before, so presumably you are charismatic enough to hold a conversation with another human with some level of skill. If this is the case, I pry open the closed mouth client by calling attention to the elephant in the room. "Jon… it is clear to me that you have some apprehension here. I want to assure you that my only goal here is to help you. Any questions I ask are really meant to move us down the path of determining if we are a right fit for each other. This isn't an 'anything you say can and will be used against you' situation. My aim is to leave you in a better position than I found you."

I'm not gonna lie, this one is not totally foolproof, but the small amount of people you alienate with a statement like this, would either not have done business with you anyway, or would have taken up five client's worth of time to make one sale. The folks who do get it will slowly loosen up. Just ask them questions that are pertinent and pull at threads. Ask these folks too many questions about that dog barking in the background or what breakfast cereal they like will shut them right back down.

With this chapter being all about shutting our face holes, there is one age-old sales maxim that I feel the need to bring up before we move on. "The first one to speak loses" has been thrown around for years. When it comes to a negotiation, it definitely holds water. When it comes to closing a deal, it works too… conditionally. You have to know your client though. Since this technique is well known, clients will often do it right back to you causing a very uncomfortable phone silence or staring contest.

Being prepared for this is important. Again, I like to de-fuse the silence with some humor.

"Louis, now is the time where you are supposed to ask me how we get everything started. This is no time to be shy. Let me grab that paperwork and I will walk you through the next steps…"

Or, you can just be matter of fact.

"It sounds like you don't have any more questions. Did you want to pay by check or take advantage of our financing options?"

I'm guessing that 75% of the time these statements will bring out further objections, which get you closer to a close. If you already earned the close though, they might just be the icebreaker needed to get them to sign on the dotted line.

# HOMEWORK

***If it's not clear to you yet that this chapter is all about listening, you probably aren't listening to the words I am typing. Ever do that? Read page after page of a book, but not pay attention at all then have to go back and re-read it all over again? Happens to me all the time. Don't do it with my books though. Get your money's worth!

Okay, back to the challenge. This challenge will be more fun if you enjoy an occasional adult beverage, but possible without one as well. I want you to go sit at a bar, alone. Your job is to extract as much info out of the bartender as you can without he/she learning too much about you. This will be hard since good bartenders do the exact opposite to you.

The challenge is to win by 7. Track it with a little tick sheet or something similarly rudimentary so you don't look like a cub reporter taking notes. If you get seven pieces of info before they get any, you win. If they ask your name or where you're from, that counts, so they score one and you must reach 8. Keep going until your score exceeds theirs by seven. At some point they will probably think you are hitting on them. Who knows, it could even end up in a date (I keep saying that sales is like dating anyway).

Complete this challenge, and it will be that much easier next time you start a conversation with a prospect when you have a common interest between you.

# FOLLOW YOUR NOES

**Follow your "Noes"**

No, sucks. We offer to buy a girl a drink and they say "no thanks" and our confidence is kicked in the nuts. Even worse, we walk back over to our buddies and they aren't exactly offering a shoulder to cry on. I liken sales to dating all the time. I always say that my greatest sale was convincing my wife to sign on the dotted line of that marriage license, knowing all of the weirdness and humanity that came with me.

If you are a man in sales, you no doubt lived through this in your youth and maybe still do. If you are a woman in sales, you either lived through this at some point or the exact opposite. I bet when you started in sales, you started to empathize with those poor saps offering to buy you a Cosmo in exchange for some polite conversation.

It's no wonder that we have this unfounded fear of hearing no. Look at your average conversion. Ratios will differ depending on your field, but I think it is safe to say that a 10-20% conversion from lead to sale is solid. This means that out of 100 people you speak to, minimum, 80 are not "yeses". Thankfully, these aren't all telling you no. A good portion won't qualify in some way shape or form to use or buy the product. We can safely put that at 50% of the noes. This leaves us with 40-45 prospects telling us, or our prospectors to take a hike. It's real. And it can be real disheartening at times.

It's a numbers game. Knowing that such a large portion of our leads will be "noes" right off the bat is both a blessing and a curse. What if the "yeses" are the LAST ten to twenty people we talk to? Even worse in the pessimist's eyes, what if the first ten people are "yeses". Will you assume the next ninety will be telling you where to shove your product? Numbers don't lie right? Why even get out of bed if we know we are going to just hear "no" all day?

In reality, it is usually, somewhere right in the middle. Our yeses will be sprinkled amongst the noes. This is why we have to learn to recognize hot and cold streaks early.

If you've ever gambled or played a competitive sport (are there non-competitive sports?), you've experienced being in the zone. You win seemingly twenty hands of Blackjack in a row, doubling down and still winning. What do you do when you lose three in a row? Do you press? Or do you recognize that the streak may be over and get up from the table with a pile of newfound chips?

You're on the basketball court and you are draining buckets like Cousin Terio left and right. Nothing is missing. So you start launching threes from just over half court. You quickly lay a few bricks. Chances are, the coach is about to pull you and give you a rest. You are starting to get in your own way!

The same thing happens to us as salespeople. We hear no on our first 7 or 8 prospects. We don't even get to present our product. It's just stonewall city and the clients just don't want to listen to what we have to say. What do we do? The very next person we talk to is already prejudged to be no #9 of the day. We just know that they are going to be an asshole. It's definitely them, how could it be us, right?

At this point, I want you to take a breather. If it's only 10 or 11 am, go to lunch or the gym. Go take a walk around Best Buy and play with video games (this always worked for me). It doesn't matter what you do; just do something. You are cancerous to your own sale at this point. Call it a morning. Come back late afternoon and start A NEW DAY. This is very important. If you cannot shake off the crap from the morning, call it a day. Same thing if it's after 1pm and you hit the dry spell. Stop putting good money after bad. You won't win.

Remember, it is a numbers game. But people also buy on emotion and energy. We've all had that day where we just knew the next prospect was signing on the dotted line. They were no match for us and they wanted the product and could afford the product. We are in the zone! Here's where you must resist the urge to celebrate your good day. Remember, a bad day is lurking around the corner, so make hay while the sun shines. Play the hot hand until you get a predetermined number of noes. Remember the guy with the hot hand in basketball. Once he hit a few bricks in a row and took some chances, coach was ready to pull him. Ride your wave until you lay those bricks.

There is a saying I like. "Don't let your highs get too high and your lows too low." Simply put, if you have a great day, don't go put money down on a Bentley and start popping Dom. You're bound to come down to earth eventually. On the flip, if you have a bad day, there is no reason to start questioning yourself or checking to see if those 10th floor windows open. You've had success in the past. You will have success again. Know it in your heart and you will find it tomorrow.

Learn to take every no as being one step closer to the next yes. I had an old Sales Manager who, despite being a racist prick, had some good advice that I have passed on to countless proteges over the years. In this job, I had to cold call teachers out of the employee phone book. I was 23 or 24 at the time and saw myself as anything but an authority. This may as well have been cleaning septic tanks as much as I hated it. So my boss made a deal with me. If I got twenty-five noes every night, I was done. How hard could that be? Just make twenty-five calls and call it an evening. Piece of cake!!!

The oddest thing happened to me though. I wasn't done in 25 calls. I was so focused on getting to the 25 noes, that I started getting "yeses"! It actually took me about 28-30 calls to get to 25 noes because I was actually finding success and booking appointments! That drunk fucker totally twisted me up. I was no longer worried about a no because I wanted a no.

Every time one of my reports or proteges complains that they can't get a yes, I toss this challenge. It is amazing how well it works. I've recently tossed it at seasoned salespeople with mindset issues. It works!

Something to keep in mind, which is actually the opposite of dating, is that when a prospect says no, they are not always saying no to <u>you</u>. They may be saying no to the company, product, or even the timing of your sale. Don't take it personally. Now, if you offer to buy a guy or a gal a drink and they flat out say no, it may be time for a stylist, or a dentist, or maybe a shower because they <u>are</u> saying no to <u>you</u>.

Something else to keep in mind is that noes and yeses are not permanent. We've all had fickle clients back out on us and leads we thought were gone forever come calling a week or two later saying "I'm ready" and leaving us scratching our heads. So don't burn that bridge.

Resist the urge to take it personal and tell a "no" where they can stick that no. Resist the urge to badmouth your competition. Let them drop the ball themselves. Not everyone is as agile as you. Some folks need to deliberate. Some need to kick the tires, put irons in the fire, mull it over, build a spreadsheet, talk to their spouse and end our call with "Well, I got your number..., I will call you.". Politely thank them for their time and set a firm follow-up. I guarantee every other schmoe they are talking to is fuming and starting to get short with them at this point (unless of course, they bought this book as well). Kill the no with kindness and a funny thing happens. You win! That same person who is blowing you off is also blowing off your less calm competition. Handle this right and increase your bottom line.

# HOMEWORK

This one is easy. Find out your conversion metrics. How many sales do you need to make in a day to hit or exceed your goal (a)? How many leads does it take you to make a sale (b)?

(a)x(b)-(a)

This is the number of noes you need to hear in a day to hit your goal.

Number a sheet of paper and tick off every "no" you get throughout the day. Make a quick note as to why your prospect did not buy. The notes are important as we can also increase conversion by finding common objections to overcome.

This is exactly the exercise I was given and have assigned countless times. Focus on hearing "no" and the "yeses" will inevitably sneak in!

# YOU'VE GOT TO BELIEVE!

**You've Got To Believe!**

My first commission sales job was great. It was the mid-nineties and I took a job selling tax sheltered annuities to folks in the education and health care field. I started off doing well enough and really enjoyed the freedom of making my own hours and truly being in charge of my own destiny.

I was partial to placing folks into a specific product offered by one of America's largest investment firms. Returns were great on this particular fund and the name recognition afforded by its firm made this a no-brainer sale that I was able to work people into a froth to get into. I mastered that one product and made it the focus of my sale. Clients ate it up. My shtick was strong and the returns were obvious.

Then, "tragedy" struck. I found out that the product I was so keen on selling was also available in the majority of my territory directly from the investment firm. This meant that my clients could reap the benefits of my pet product while cutting out the middleman (me) and save themselves hundreds, potentially thousands in maintenance and transaction fees.

Finding this out crushed my confidence. I had spent the previous six months or so, honing the sale on this product to the point of selling myself thoroughly on it. In my eyes, there was no other product as powerful for my clients. The problem was, I started to believe that I was irrelevant. Why did they need me if they could get it cheaper elsewhere.

Looking back, I know that I was the differentiator. When they cut out the middleman, they also cut out the adviser and were left to their own devices to manage their retirement funds. I really was worth the extra cost (an extra cost mind you, that the client usually didn't even know existed), but twenty-five year old me was too naive to see that. All I saw was that I was "screwing" the client by not telling them about the direct option.

My ability to sell that product was lost, because I no longer believed it was the best for the client. I never recovered from this. Anytime I found a new fund to push, all I saw were the reasons my company was non-essential to the client in the process.

This is why I want you to find a way to believe in what you are selling. Customers can sense when you are "selling" them. They can tell when you don't care. But when you can genuinely demonstrate that you not only understand the problem you are solving for them, but also fully believe that your product will help, they will feel it and ultimately buy your product.

At the same time, one trap I want you to never fall into is lying to the customer. Telling them you use your product when you really don't is not only unethical, but it is also transparent. You will eventually be found out. Losing your integrity as a salesperson is the kiss of death.

**Dogfooding**

Dogfooding is a great way to get to know your product and build the familiarity with how it adds benefit to your life. Many companies encourage their employees to "eat their own dog food".

This term is said to have originated from one of two places. The first possible origin is from the original Alpo Dog Food commercials where spokesman Lorne Greene pointed out that he fed Alpo to his own dogs. The second, less appetizing origin story comes from Kal Kan Dog Food, where the president of the company was rumored to start shareholder' meetings off by chowing down on a bowl of Kal Kan.

Regardless of the back-story, a manager at Microsoft in the late nineties by the name of Paul Maritz is credited for a now famous email where he encouraged Microsoft employees to "Eat our own dogfood" and increase internal usage of Microsoft's products.

Regardless of where the term comes from, dogfooding is invaluable. Who better to sell a product than a satisfied customer? You become even more of a trusted adviser in this respect. How easy is it to get a friend to binge-watch a TV show that you love? Your enthusiasm for House of Cards or Game of Thrones is infectious and gets them excited to watch it themselves. Your seal of approval goes far! On the flip side, your seal of disapproval holds even more weight. Think about the faces we make when offered a food we can't stand. That grimace far outweighs the face we make when offered our favorite treat. People are more demonstrative about things that bring them pain.

One such story I have about lying about the product takes it to the extreme. Years ago, I was in a training class for a position in the mortgage industry. A friend of mine was in that very same class.

As part of our training, we were coached on live calls with potential prospects. My buddy was building great rapport with a potential client and due to his inexperience, he was circling around the loan products he was putting together for the client and the client was questioning it. The trainer who was working with him had him put the prospect on hold and told my buddy to say "This is the product for you. It is the one I have on my own mortgage right now". The problem was, my buddy was NOT a homeowner. He was renting and did not yet own his own home. He uncomfortably got back on the phone and to his credit, he did not use the line he was told to use. In the end, he did not earn the client's business that day, but he did earn the client's trust. We will never know how that story ends though, because there was never a follow-up as my friend handed in his resignation the next day because he did not feel comfortable with being encouraged to lie to a potential client.

If it is not possible for you to use your product yourself due to you not being the target market or any other reason, you can still find many ways to build your belief in the product. Client testimonials are a great way to see what past customers have said about the product. These customer reviews are great for helping you figure out what features offered what benefit for customers. As well as building your confidence in knowing that your product really did do the trick for folks.

Knowing all of the features and benefits of your product is key to this. You need to understand why a customer needs your product and why they should want the product as well. Uncovering their need will help you tailor your explanation of how the features will benefit them. Once the customer grasps the reason they want it, their need then becomes having the product. Our job is turning that initial need into want.

Picture your perfect customer avatar. What are the top 5 problems they are solving with your product? Each customer might have one unique reason for needing the product, but figure out the top five reasons that will bring people through the door.

Now match up one of the features of your product with each of those top five. Take careful notes. To be clear, this is not your sale. This is the outline of what you must know in order to hone your presentation.

Now, take each of those features and write a paragraph or two about the benefit they will receive from said feature. From here, your sales pitch is taking shape. To the average car buyer, the navigation package is merely a four-figure line item in an ever expanding list of features that inflate the cost of their car. When they hear the story of how one of your favorite clients got turned around on a back road in Hazzard County and was able to utilize the non-cellular dependent satellite navigation system to find their way back to the highway, and make it to their only granddaughter's graduation on time, it paints a picture.

Reaching out to past customers for testimonials like these is a great practice. Not only do you get usable material for your future sales calls, but you also show them that you do care about them after the sale. Don't forget to ask for referrals!

This is not our last discussion of features vs. benefits, as we will certainly talk about them more in this and subsequent books. Knowing the benefits will help you gain the belief in your product that you need to sell effectively.

# HOMEWORK

Take a few minutes and write down your favorite TV show, movie, food, and social destination. Over the course of the next week, I want you to convince (not sell) a friend, co-worker or family member to try each of these for themselves.

Assess each conversation afterward. What types of words did you use? How did your voice sound? At what point in the conversation did you sense that you had convinced them to try it out?

If you took this assignment seriously, you chose something you already had passion for, so selling someone on trying it out is not that difficult. Take the enthusiasm, tone and words you used in this exercise and apply it to your sales presentation.

# DON'T BE A LYMAN

**Make friends with them. Don't just sell them.**

It's a fact that people will by from someone they like. One of the easiest ways to prove this is looking at the opposite statement for corroboration. People will rarely buy from someone they don't' like. Ever met a top salesperson that was a total dick? If so, did you observe them around their clients? I bet they were the exact opposite when in the zone. They flip the switch and become super personable when it counts. This is important. The key is, to be genuine.

Customers are already on guard. Being patronizing, pedantic, or fake is super transparent. Remember, our prospects are on high alert at first and really have no reason to trust us, so odds are they won't until we earn it. If their spider sense is already activated and we are fake to them, they will pick up on it immediately.

How do we make friends in our day-to-day lives? We find common ground. I can't tell you how many games of Jewish Geography I took part in growing up, where we figured out who we knew in common 'Six Degrees of Kevin Bacon' style. Whether it's a common friend or a shared interest, it is easy to make friends when we relate to the person we are interacting with in some way.

One way to put them at ease is to humanize yourself. Put them on equal ground. When we approach a strange dog, we offer them a limp hand to show them we mean no harm. We should be doing the same with our customers. One way I do this with my clients (which is sadly all too real) is apologizing up front for a cough or losing my voice due to allergies kicking in. A good 80% of my prospects acknowledge that they too feel my pain. Whoah! Just like that, we are brothers in arms. A few tasteful self-deprecating jokes tossed in, along with a humble brag or two "Yeah, they make the old guys like me work from home so the young kids don't know what kind of pricing we get for our clients." and we're in. Answer their questions properly, show them what they want and close.

A topic to avoid starting a conversation with is weather. It's a straight up tee-ball conversation and odds are, your competition is using it as well. It's not a topic to avoid altogether, since it is top of mind, but if I hear you say, "How's the weather up there?" on a phone call, you will instantly lose 10 charisma points.

One trap that is super important to avoid is being too nice. That guy who is a dick at the office and suave with his clients has this mastered. He/She earns their customers respect and trust through knowledge and mastery while earning their like by humanizing themselves and entertaining the prospect. He/She displays that they will confidently go to war for their clients… and win.

If we are too nice and accommodating we turn ourselves into a Lyman; Lyman is a guy I worked with years ago. He was handsome, funny, a great dancer and kind beyond belief. Lyman's achilles heel is that folks liked him a ton, but had no respect for him. Prospects had no issue saying no to Lyman. And he had no problem saying "OK" to their no. He hadn't earned the right to be the master and expert.

We all work for our clients, but Lyman turned himself into their employee. Along these same lines, Lyman had trouble keeping clients because they were not afraid to call him after they initially said yes and back out of a deal. They were right not to be afraid, because he really did just say "OK" to them when they called him back with the lamest of excuses. He never fought back and poked holes in their flawed logic. He just took it. If we have done our job correctly, the clients should have some fear of calling us to back out because they know we will merely remind them off all the reasons they said yes to begin with. Our job is to sell them and re-sell them. If we let them back out after saying yes, remind them of what life is like without your product. Don't be a Lyman.

# HOMEWORK

You get to watch TV for homework! Watch an episode or two from an earlier season, then a later season of Entourage. If you haven't ever watched the show, I recommend it. For about $15, you can have HBO on demand for a month and a copy of this book. What a great investment in your career!

In the earlier season, look at the difference between how Ari and Lloyd are perceived by their clients. Ari's clients have absolute faith that he is going to bust down doors and negotiate on their behalf to a serious win. Ari also burns many bridges in doing his job. This scorched earth mentality can be very detrimental.

Lloyd on the other hand gets pushed around and is not taken seriously by his clients or his business associates. Both often go over his head and call Ari. They do not trust he can get the job done.

As the show progresses and the characters evolve, Ari begins to grow a heart. People start to see the good in him and he sacrifices a bit of his bullishness to show some vulnerability that ultimately pays dividends.

On the opposite end of the spectrum, Lloyd grows some more balls. He learns when and how to take control of the situation and his clients. This gives him more of an aura of invincibility which pays off when he shows his clients what he is capable of and grows.

You need to learn when to be an Ari and when to be a Lloyd. And never, under any circumstances, be a Lyman.

# SET GOAL-DI-LOCKS

**Don't aim too low or too high. Aim just right.**

Goals are important. Without intelligent goal setting, we have nothing to aim for and no direction. As salespeople, the vast majority of us are the masters or mistresses of our own domain. We dictate how well we do and how hard we push. We may have a manager or team lead, but for the most part, we are our own boss. Improperly setting goals is a major way that we sabotage our business.

The first danger in goal setting is setting our goals too high. Everyone wants to succeed, and face it, if we didn't want to make more money, we'd find an easier salary job to settle into. In this respect it is all too easy to sit down at the beginning of a month, quarter or year and set an outrageous goal to shoot for. These goals are great because they give us something to shoot for that is beyond our normal reach. You must build your sales muscle to get there.

Much like lifting weights though, very few of us can walk into a gym, say "I'm going to bench press 300 pounds", lie down on the bench and toss it up. You have to first test your own tolerance for what you can lift and gradually build up to heavier weights. If you set proper incremental goals, you can work up to that 300lb lift in time.

Goal setting for sales is very much the same. You have to first get your baseline and see what you can achieve on a daily / weekly / monthly and extrapolate goals from there. Ratchet these up accordingly and you will eventually get to levels you never believed you could achieve.

Try to bench press 300lbs when you have never lifted seriously before, and you will more than likely get hurt; both physically and your pride. In the same vein, set your sales goals too high and you will not only hurt your pride, but it creates a losing mindset. In our business, mindset plays such a huge role. It can make or break you. We need wins, even small ones, along the way to keep the right mindset. Don't get me wrong, missing a goal here and there doesn't make you a loser, but at the same time, purposely setting goals we know we will miss by a landslide does no good.

Setting goals that we are sure to miss does something else to our mindset. We start to rationalize missing goals. Once it becomes "OK" to not hit a goal because "I knew it wasn't attainable, I just did it to stretch myself", it starts to creep in that any goal we set is not firm. When we start to see goals as suggestions, mediocrity enters our life.

On the other end, setting goals that are too easy gives us a lot of little wins, but we end up not growing. Think of the weightlifter that never challenges himself or the chubby guy who gets on the treadmill and goes the same time/distance/speed every day (yeah… I am looking in the mirror). They may lose weight, but progress will be much slower than if they challenge themselves.

When our goals are too attainable, it becomes all too easy to start strong and taper off. We allow ourselves to slack knowing that we are so close to the goal that we can coast. Have you ever had that month where on the 20th, you are pacing to exceed a goal then inexplicably on the 30th, you are scrambling to find more business to make it to the goal? You are not alone, this happens all the time. It occurs because we let it. Our goal was small enough that we fool ourselves into thinking we don't have to try.

Similarly, setting goals too low stunts are growth. We grow complacent with hitting the easy goal and the false positive we get from it. Once this occurs, we begin to rationalize our business and build our own glass ceiling. Our mindset then has us fooled into thinking we are capped at this attainable goal and we never stretch.

You might be thinking, "Are you crazy Scott?" We can't set goals too high and we can't set them too low. How do we find that Goldilocks level?

Much like that weightlifter, we have to find out what we are capable of at a baseline first. Once you have a baseline, you can ratchet it up to achieve growth. Pull your numbers for the last quarter. What did you do per day/week/month? It's safe to say that since you have done it, it's possible.

Now figure out what you want your increase to be? What is possible? What did the top producer in the company do? It is also safe to assume that this is also possible. Are you as experienced as they are? Do they possess something you don't? This is what I mean by not reaching TOO high. If someone has already done it, it is possible. If they can do it, so can you. If you feel that this goal is the equivalent of that 300lb bench press, set your initial goal right in between what you did and what the top producer did and increase accordingly as you hit milestones along the way.

What if you are brand new at the company and have no metrics to go on? Again, look at what other folks have produced most recently. Do you feel that you have what it takes to be #1 out of the gate? If so, aim for the top. If not, take the top ten producers and find where the cliff is. Where is there a large jump in #s? If the number 6 performer far out-produces 7-10, set your sights on beating #6. Look at the entire top ten in this way. If the cliff is between #3 and #4, make #3 your rabbit and chase them.

Now... What if you are in the enviable position of being the top performer already? Remember, everyone below you is gunning for you, so you won't stay number one for long if you stay stat quo. You must set goals that will help you grow your business and income. This is a point where I like to have fun with goals. Chances are, if you are at the top already, you are making a fine living for yourself. Set a goal that allows you to reward yourself. What will this increase in sales for the month, quarter or year allow you to do that might be outside of your normal spending zone? Down payment on a vacation home? Serious upgrade in the automotive department? Maybe the big daddy Rolex? Money can't buy happiness, but it sure can buy some cool stuff. And cool stuff can seriously alter your mindset to the positive, which can then increase your bottom line and earn you even more money.

Once you set your realistic goals, it is time to break them down. Take your quarterly goal and break it down to monthly goals. Evaluate this. Is it a stretch, yet attainable? Is it an increase over what you have been doing? If so, skip weekly goals and go directly to daily. This is hugely important because every month has different amounts of business days and holidays. Be sure to take into account any planned vacation time (if you are not taking any vacation time, please start doing do immediately). Divide your monthly goal by actual business days. Is this daily number a stretch, yet attainable? Good!

We are almost there.

Pull out your calendar and figure out where you need to be each Friday to hit your goal. Now is where we will mind-fuck ourselves a bit. Take ALL of your Friday goals and multiply them by 1.1. "Wait, you told us to keep our goals attainable and not overreach. This is counter intuitive." I hear you. But we are out to grow our business remember? I've been a little soft on you and chances are, you played it a little safe so far. What is a ten percent increase really? If you normally make two sales a day, that's ten a week. Increasing that by ten percent is ONE MORE SALE. That extra sale is gravy. Remember, we are NOT increasing your monthly or quarterly goals one iota. With thirteen weeks in the quarter, if you hit that extra one sale every other week you are ensured not to be scrambling at the last minute. In fact, you'd only have to make four sales in that last week to hit your goal. If you were able to hit the extra ten percent EVERY week, you'll blast through your goal a full week early.

This is a numbers game. It is important to see things not only as a marathon, but also a series of small sprints that make up the race. When you break down your quarter, know that you will have strong days/weeks/months and weak ones to boot. Proper goal setting will allow you to earn the living you desire without the stress of scrambling to hit the goal. As an added benefit, not having that last minute stress means you don't have to sound desperate in the end. Clients smell fear and when you are pressuring them after the 25th of a month, they know they have the upper hand as you are trying to hit your goal.

# HOMEWORK

Sit down and map out your yearly, quarterly, monthly, weekly and daily goals. Once you have them clearly laid out, find an accountability partner who you can do scheduled check-ins with. Put these check-ins in your calendar and do not miss them.

Your partner is merely there to check on you. They do not have to coach you if they/you do not want. Hit a goal? Celebrate with a high-five and keep running to stay ahead of pace for the next milestone. Miss a goal? Question the why, but don't dwell on it. Make adjustments to subsequent goals and move on. Remember, you are focusing on these mile markers toward your ultimate destination.

# NO PERFECT TIME

**There is no perfect time**

One other way we get in our own way is waiting for the perfect time to call a client and even worse, the perfect time to close.

No one wants to look like they are just sitting by the phone waiting for your call. How often do you call on a prospect that is just "hanging out"? They want to sound busy. Think about all the times you catch someone who is on a conference call, in a meeting or "just walking into a meeting". Let's just agree to something here. One, if you are ON a conference call, you aren't putting it on hold to take a random sales call. Two, if you are in a meeting, you aren't calling time-out to take a call on your cell. And three, look at your watch the next time you say you are walking into a meeting. We know meetings don't start promptly at 11:18 am these days.

With that little rant out of the way, never wait around for the perfect time to call. Does the following sound familiar?

We don't want to call before 9am because they are in traffic.

We don't want to call between nine and ten because they are just starting their day.

We call around ten-thirty and they are engrossed in whatever they started doing at 9:30. They want a call at lunch.

We call during lunch and get voice mail.

We don't want to call right after lunch because we know they will be busy with returning their calls and emails from lunch and the morning.

So we wait until two-ish in the afternoon to call. By this time, we are lethargic and frustrated with "chasing them" even though WE created the chase and procrastinations. They pick up and when they sound busy, we offer the objection of calling after five.

We call at 5:15 as promised while they are in the car and get voice mail because they got stuck in the office. So we decide to call back tomorrow, rinse, repeat.

What you must do instead is call first thing. If they are busy, they will tell you. Book a solid time for a follow up. If you get them to commit to a time, you can hold them accountable when they miss it and they will respect you. They also won't repeat the missing of appointments. You will gain that valuable meeting and more than likely a new client, all because you did not give yourself the excuse.

To me, closing a sale is a lot like dating. Along those same lines, the first close is like the first kiss. There are few things more awkward than that first date where you have the jitters all night. She's wondering if you are going to make a move, you're trying to figure out all night how to be smooth and say the right thing at the right time with the right light and lean in for that movie kiss. In reality what happens is either an awkward hug/handshake/peck, a completely out of context mauling or in many cases the drinks kind of "make it happen" and you really don't have rhyme or reason.

Imagine, if when you picked her up you said "Here's how I'd like to see the night go. I am going to take you to a nice dinner and we'll finish off a nice bottle of Pinot. Then we'll hit that new Rom Com and I'll probably try to hold your hand a little. I might even do the yawn that turns into an arm around the shoulders. After the movie, maybe we'll grab a nightcap and I will walk you to your door. Provided I haven't made an ass of myself, I will take that moment to steal my first kiss with you."

Now if she had an objection to that foreshadow of the evening, she might just let you know right away. If she doesn't, it is safe to assume that things will progress as stated unless otherwise interrupted with texts from a sick friend or you getting slapped for saying something inappropriate. At the end of the night, you will be feeling pretty confident as you walk her to the door. There might even be an Air Supply song playing in your head as the lighting is indeed perfect and you get that kiss just like in the movie you saw earlier.

Closing is just like that kiss! If you take the time to foreshadow how your sales presentation will go, the client cannot be or even act surprised when you walk over to them with Air Supply playing in your head and lean in for that open mouthed close. How can they? You mapped out exactly what you were going to do up front. They knew that you were going to present your product or service to them and that they would have ample time to ask questions as you deftly answered them and handled all objections before going in for the kill. If they had an objection, they had every opportunity to stop you beforehand. You are home free. All you need to do is ask for the business!

Of course, I am over simplifying things a bit. Simply

foreshadowing the date is not going to turn you into instant Clooney. I will tell you though that going in blind, tentative and sweaty-pitted like you have in the past is a one-way trip to handshake city.

Likewise, you still have work to do between the start of your sales call and the first close, but you will be infinitely more confident as you go through the steps of your sale. That first close is also, not a guaranteed panty dropper, but at that point, your objections turn into buying signs in disguise. Handle an objection, close again. At this point, if they are not interested, they will find a way to shut you down. If they don't, repeat the process until you have exhausted their objections and they are ready to sign on the line.

Remember, just like she said yes to that date, the prospect is there for a reason. They are interested in buying your product. They wouldn't have taken the meeting otherwise. This means they enter the meeting leaning toward "yes". How we handle ourselves and the presentation can either get them leaning further that way or push them in the other direction. Knowing that they start off on our side, that proper foreshadow can set the tone. Get them further on our side of the Prime Meridian and any stumbles on our end won't push them back over the line.

# HOMEWORK

Start utilizing this in your daily life outside of work. Find at least three other avenues in your life where a powerful foreshadow can sway things in our favor. Put that foreshadowing to good use.

I will share two ways my wife does this to me:

1. On Friday evening, she lays out her rough plans for her/us for the weekend. She is laying it all out there in case I have any objections up front. If I do, we adjust accordingly. If not, it is assumed the plan is OK.

2. If she wants to make a large purchase, she uses the "start high" method. "I saw this couch I wanted to buy, but it was way too expensive. $10,000 for a couch isn't something I can justify." She just leaves this out there to float in space. It's a seemingly innocuous statement right? She's setting a subconscious baseline for me. A week or so later, I am primed for the setup when she says, "I am super excited. I found a couch similar to that $10,000 one and this one is only $4,000!" She has put that still expensive $4,000 couch on sale without it even being on sale.

I hope husbands and wives alike can both benefit from #2.

# DON'T FORGET TO CLOSE

**Don't forget to close**

Would you ever consider working a full week then tell your boss to just keep the paycheck? Of course you wouldn't. Occasionally, as salespeople, we do just this. We prospect, we set appointments, we pitch, and then we set a follow-up, all without closing. Just like working that forty-hour week, going through the entire sales process without actually asking for the business is one of the dumbest things we do to get in our own way as sales folks, yet we do it every day.

Not closing comes from a few places. All of which can be addressed and tweaked in your game.

One such place not closing comes from is not recognizing when the client is ready. This can be a tough one. Very rarely does the prospect ask us "So... what's the next step from here?".

We must learn to recognize buying signs, both subtle and otherwise. If it's in person and you are pitching to more than one person, one such cue is when one client looks at the other and gives the head tilt and eyebrow as if to say "What do you think?". At this point, that non-verbal can either mean one of them is on board, both is on board or the slightly worse, neither on board. At the end of the day, it really doesn't matter, because a trial close here flushes that all out. If one is on board, you now have a sales assistant and someone to bounce things off at the other. If the trial close reveals that both are on board, you merely have to follow up with a major call to action "Sounds like everything is in order, let me fill you in on the process from here and we'll get everything rolling." If none of them are on board, the trial close offers you the opportunity to handle their objections. Responding relevantly and closing again will push you one step closer to having that aforementioned sales assistant.

When selling over the phone, one great buying sign to me is the first question that does not involve price. I like to get the price objection out of the way early by letting them know I will work with them and ensure they get the best pricing available. Everyone wants to know price because it is always a concern. I like when they ask me other questions like "What's the turn time?" or "Would we be able to tweak it like this?" At this point it's easy to toss a close out there with a call to action to get any final objections out. "We certainly could alter the payment plan to your needs. Let's go ahead and get everything started and if you change your mind on the payment terms tomorrow, we can make that switch at your request on the fly without skipping a beat." This second part will take away the objection of "OK, I will think about which way to go tonight and call you tomorrow." They've told us they want to work with us, that final piece is all that needs to be ironed out and it is the tiniest of speed bumps. No roadblocks in sight.

Of course, these are just a few generic ways to recognize that the window to closing is open. I cannot give definitive buying signs for all products, industries and situations. It's up to you to reflect back on your past sales calls to see where exactly those magic moments occurred. Hindsight is 20/20 here. It's also so much easier to recognize when it is time to close when you are not the salesperson. As a leader of sales teams, I learned to recognize the simplest non-verbal cues even without hearing both sides of the call. I could be caught waving my arms multiple times a day mouthing "CLOSE!" to my proteges even without knowing what the client on the other end of the phone was saying. You can feel the ebb and flow of the sales call just from the rhythm of the conversation.

Get me on the phone with my own clients however, and I sometimes miss simple buying signs while trying to dazzle the client with my knowledge and advice. Sometimes these things are not so visible when you are in the bubble.

I am beginning to think I may have hung with the wrong crowd as a younger man, because I have yet another quote given to me by a co-worker years ago about not knowing when to close. "You've got her lying there naked in the bed waiting and you're wasting time blowing out candles dummy." Yeah... crass, but true. Once the client is ready to buy, we can easily talk them right out of the sale.

Continue to talk when the client is ready to go, and we run the risk of feeding them objections or giving them reason to think. Every feature/benefit we give at that point has them wondering if this is really what they want or if company x down the road can do that thing better. Buyer's remorse sets in regardless. The more we bullshit with them without moving the sale forward, the higher the chances of that remorse hitting before they even buy!

Learn to recognize buying signs and capitalize. Learning when to close is something that comes with time, but when you figure out these sweet spots, your job gets that much easier. Pay attention and learn! Don't worry about the candles. If she wants them blown out, she'll let you know.

# HOMEWORK

Practice makes perfect. If we find ourselves avoiding or "forgetting" the close, we must get more comfortable doing so.

Your homework is to close on every call/meeting for a week. Do not leave the room or end a call without closing in some way shape or form. Do not take no for an answer. Do not take the second no for an answer. The third no is discretionary. Do you feel you can convert the prospect? Set a follow up or close again. Is this a dead end? The third no earns you your exit.

Some of you hotshots out there are probably saying "I already do this, why wouldn't I close on every sales call?" I guarantee this is not the case. You are definitely prejudging some prospects and not seeing the benefit yourself, so you are letting the client (and yourself) off easy. EVERY SINGLE presentation this week gets closed.

Not seeing the benefit? Find one. The prospect took the meeting for a reason. State your benefit and close. Is the client trying to end the conversation abruptly? CLOSE! Make them give you an objection. If they are shooting you down, you didn't earn the close to begin with. That objection will take the conversation in the right direction.

Play your cards right this week and a few things will happen. First, you will make a couple of sales you didn't expect because you merely asked for the business. How's that for a confidence boost? Second, you will grow more and more comfortable with closing and responding to objections, which in turn will earn you more sales. Lastly, by finding success where you saw "noes" before, you will turbo charge your business and increase your conversion rate.

# FINAL THOUGHTS

"Those who can't do, teach."

We've all heard it before. Shit, I've said it on more than one occasion. This statement was embodied for a generation by Tom Cruise's professor in the movie Cocktail. I've come across sales coaches that couldn't hold my jock on the sales floor and probably gave them less respect than they deserved just for trying to do their job.

Don't get it twisted,I didn't write this book in penance for disrespecting some poor sap in the past though. I wrote this book to help you... and to help me. I am a player-coach in the truest sense of the word, on the field day in and day out overcoming objections with the best and worst of you. We're in the foxhole together, working to keep my own mindset in check as I navigate waters both rough and smooth.

Another reason I was compelled to write this book is in direct response to some of the "Sales Tips" I have seen recently. I have seen so many "Mini-Wolves of Wall Street" lately sharing their successes. In my eyes, we don't have to channel high-pressure salesman from the big screen to excel in our field. It's not about pounding Red Bull and chest-bumping after we "bag a sale". Do your job right, and everybody wins.

Sales is in my blood. I cannot escape it. By harnessing it and paying it forward, I can make a difference. If I can earn each of you an extra sale, if I can get you past an objection, if I can save you from stressing out, I will consider this effort a success.

Take the lessons in this book, use them and share them. It's time to get out of your own way and find success.

# THE 30 MINUTE SALES COACH PRESENTS...

**Sell Even Smarter**

Seven More Simple Strategies for Sales Success

*This book is dedicated to my beautiful wife Beth.*

*Without you, I would still be a 12 year old in a man's body. You are the very definition of "Better Half".*

*You are amazing.*

# I'M JUST BROWSING

I have a story to share. I am going to go out on a limb here and assume you have been to a Best Buy before. What's the first thing that happens when you go into a Best Buy (after the security person gives you their "I know you're here" greeting)? The same thing that happens in nearly any good retail store. They ask you if they can help you find something.

So here I am, walking into Best Buy on the day *The Dark Knight Rises* is released on Blu Ray. Not that I will watch it on a Tuesday night, but I had to have it on that first day for some reason.

I blow by the guy at the security desk with a "Howyadoin'?" and beeline for the Blu Ray section. This was going to be a quick trip! On my way to the movie section, a blue shirt asks me if they can help me find something. "No thanks, I'm good" I respond as I find my target area.

Then it happens. I find all of the Batman movies, but no *Dark Knight Rises*. "Anything I can help you with?", another blue shirt asks. I confidently shrug them off. I know my alphabet and we are working in alphabetical order. How hard can it be to find? I keep looking. NOTHING. I check the end cap. NOTHING.

At this point, I have already acted like a cocky know-it-all, so I don't want to concede that I need help.

Then it hits me. It's a new release. The new release movies are right up front to make them easier to find. I walked right past it while the security guy was distracting me by being polite!

I briskly walk up, grab my movie and pay. My five-minute trip took twenty.

To add a funny twist to this already all-too-true story, I didn't even watch the movie for about six months. Next time, Amazon Prime baby!

I had a point here. As humans, we have defense mechanisms. Somehow, it is ingrained in us to give the "just looking" response to salespeople. We ALL do it.

Let's look at how much easier my trip to Best Buy could have been. Had I just asked the first person to engage with me where I could find that particular movie, I'd have been in and out in 4 minutes. Instead, it took me five times as long to get through the process of doing it myself and being that guy who won't ask for directions.

Your prospects are the same way. No one wants to be perceived as "easy", so they play hard to get up front. Even if they want to buy, they don't want to be sold.

Salespeople are slimy. They are not to be trusted. If one should engage you in conversation, look away and tell them you are just looking.

The point here is that this is NOT an objection. This is merely a defense mechanism. I walked in the store right? I moved quickly to my perceived destination no? I was there to buy something. I just needed help.

What can we do to make our prospects more comfortable and

minimize this?

First, assume that everyone you talk to is going to give you the old "Just browsin'". The sooner you come to grips with this, the better. Once you do this, it becomes a greeting, just like saying "Hello".

Now, we may align ourselves with the customer. A sales conversation should be walking in the same direction, hand on shoulder, leading them to the desired outcome with warm fuzzies. Instead, we often turn it into a head-to-head game of verbal ping-pong that leads to adversarial feelings.

Try this, "You know, we rearrange the stock all the time. This place is like a giant Rubik's Cube sometimes. Let me point you in the right direction. What can I help you find?"

Note that we didn't get cocky or sales-y with that question. Remember, people are wary of salespeople. We have to prove our worth to them before they will let us in.

Don't get me wrong. It may not be quite this easy to get someone to open up, but we have to try. If we let "I'm just looking", stonewall us, we are in the wrong profession. Find the problem they are trying to solve and offer them a solution as a consultant.

Vacuum cleaner broke? "I've got what the doctor ordered. We've got some great floor models on sale and even some of those high-end robot vacuums. You don't have to spend a ton to have clean floors."

Finally wore through the soles of those Italian loafers? "Let me see if we can get those repaired for you at a reasonable price. If not, we still stock them or we even have similar shoes with more durable soles that are even more inexpensive."

Always remember, your clients are in front of you for a reason. It is up to us to figure out the problem they want to solve and help them solve it in a way they perceive to be best for them.

Take the shoe example above. Personally, I have paid 75% of the retail cost of a pair of shoes just to get them professionally resoled. I do this because I know the shoes fit, they are worn in already, and the shoemaker I go to refurbishes them like a boss. I get a BETTER pair of shoes than if I was to buy a brand new pair.

Some of my friends think I am crazy. They would gladly pay that extra 25% for a brand new pair of shoes. Are they wrong? Am I? No… and No. We just perceive the best solutions to the same problem to be differing.

In summary, expect to hear the equivalent of "I'm just looking" every time you meet a new prospect. Even if it is out of context, they will use it anyway because to them it is in context of a conversation with a salesperson. This is regardless of if it fits the transaction or not.

Once you come to grips with the fact that this is a given, you will be able to spend more time and energy overcoming the real objections that come your way.

# HOMEWORK

I hope you like to shop, because this homework assignment requires lots of it.

Your job here is to go to the mall and shop for "gifts".

To complete this assignment, you must go into at least ten stores. In each store, you will answer the first off for help with the "Just browsing" brush off.

Once you give that initial stiff-arm, allow the next person to help you and tell them you are looking for a gift for someone appropriate to the store's clientele. Take mental note of the questions they ask you in order to narrow down the perfect gift. How deep do they go? How would you change their approach.

As you leave each store, take notes in your phone or on a notepad. How did the staff at each store score? Did anyone blast through the initial "Just looking" and move right in to help?

What are your takeaways from each store, and who did the best? I want you to implement the good in your own game. If you recognize something that you do that doesn't work, remove it from your repertoire.

# "NO" IS JUST THE BEGINNING

Sometimes we have the perfect sales meeting. We seemingly hit every hurdle in stride and deftly handle objections before they are even brought up. With meetings like this, we are so on our game, there is no way we can lose. We are Superman, Rambo and Gordon Gecko rolled into one.

As great as you know you are though, I am here to let some air out of your tires. If you got absolutely no objections and they just hopped in the boat, it was probably less than half sales skill and mostly the fact that they just wanted to buy.

Don't get me wrong. After nearly twenty years selling the same market-driven product, I have been through my fair share of muffin markets. You know what I'm talking about. Suddenly, you get to work and there are free muffins in the kitchen. Your VP is bringing in lunch three times a week and your sales manager is all about buying dinner for those willing to "stick around, hustle and grind". They don't mind the extra expense because there is more revenue to go around. And if you stick around there's even more. Everybody wins!

In a muffin market, you become an order taker. Demand is high for your product and the price is right. All you really need to do is not offend the customer too badly and they'll buy from you. As a salesperson, you have to love the muffin market. Don't get it twisted though because you are not selling here. You are wearing the hat of a glorified cashier. Don't get this twisted either. It's OK to just take orders and cash some fat checks once in a while. You earned it those weeks where you pounded the pavement or phones just to make a sale. Make that hay!

Remember this. The salesperson's job doesn't start until that first objection. This is where the sale begins. Up until that point, we are tour guides and spokesmodels. We are giving features and benefits. We are kissing hands and shaking babies. We are hopefully moving the conversation toward a sale. But we are not selling yet.

Once we hear "I'll run this by my boss", "I have to talk to my wife", "OK, let me see how this fits into the budget", or something of the sort, it's game time. This is where we earn that commission. How you react is what separates you, the sales professional, from the cashier.

I love when that first objection comes out. It tells me the prospect is engaged in the conversation. Ever try driving on fresh ice? Chances are you didn't get very far because there was no friction. Without friction, the wheels just spin on the smooth surface. To me, that first objection is like sprinkling kitty litter or salt under my tires. The conversation can now begin to move in the proper direction.

It has often been said that objections are just buying signs in disguise. This is so true. A true objection gives you that hurdle to overcome on your way to a sale. Get past the smokescreen objections; uncover their true objection and close!

The problem I have seen with those frictionless sales calls is that you often don't know if you're making a ghost sale or not. Is the client putting up no fight and "yessing" us just to get off the phone or end the meeting, or are they the one who wants our product or service no matter what?

In an instance like this, I suggest doing the unthinkable. Offer them an objection. This is a simple litmus test. If they are buying no matter what, this can have a strange effect. I have had clients in these situations start selling me on them buying from me. The effect is similar to "The Takeaway Close". Clients will literally start giving you all the reasons they need/want your product no matter what. At this point, it's time to write up a contract or ring them up. Don't talk your way out of a sale!

By the same token, if the client was not a sure thing, offering them an objection like "Of course, we want to make sure your spouse is on board before we get this started right?", gives you an opportunity to really take their temperature and test the water. If they were indeed just being polite, they will jump at the chance to end the call and go on with their day.

It is important that no matter what objection we offer up though, we are prepared to test if they are a true no-shot or a maybe. We must be locked and loaded with a relevant response and close.

This second test will allow you to cut bait on those prospects who were never going to come through anyway. I don't know about you, but I would much rather hear a definitive "no" and politely say goodbye than to waste valuable time and energy following up on dead ends. Sometimes folks are too weak to tell you "no" because they don't want to hurt your feelings.

On the other side, if there is indeed some sliver of a shot, you will find it here. Remember, that first objection is a buying sign in disguise. It doesn't matter if you fed it to them or not. It is a tool to get the ball rolling in the right direction. Feed the objection, overcome it and close. What happens next? Do they just magically say "yes"? If so, your job is done, but get them signing fast. That lack of friction is still a symptom. Do they give you another objection? GOOD! Rinse and repeat until you have a "yes", a "no" or a firm follow-up with a relevant reason for follow up and all decision making parties scheduled to be present.

Remember, there is nothing wrong with a lie-down sale every once in a while and nothing wrong with just taking orders in a muffin market. Make hay while the sun shines. Just know that if you want to call yourself a sales professional, you have to S E L L.

# HOMEWORK

The homework for this chapter is simple yet might take some time.

Over the next two days, take notes of all the simple objections you hear that you can combat with ease. There should be at least five.

Rank them in order of difficulty 1-5.

Now list all of the ways you can overcome these objections. By the time you are done, you should have supreme confidence in getting past each and every one of them.

Type this list out and commit it to memory. This is your list of "traps" that you will set for the client. When you sense there is an objection lurking and you can't flush it out of them, toss out one of these softballs. They will take the bait and object. Then you swoop in and counter the objection followed by a swift close.

At this point, you will either make a sale, or force out the real objection they had. Now you have a real objection to work with. Overcome this and you are home free!

# I'LL QUIT PROCRASTINATING... TOMORROW

We've all had that one prospect for whom procrastinating is seemingly their hobby.

It's natural. An object at rest tends to stay at rest, right? Therefore, it is sometimes darn near impossible to get some of these folks to stop procrastinating.

1. It's important to recognize the why behind the behavior here.First off, the prospective customer has lived their life so far without your product. That would lead one to believe that your product is not essential to their existence.

2. Second, although folks want tobuy, they don't necessarily want to besold.

3. Lastly, they must be shown the value we are bringing them and the benefit of our product.

Let's tackle these in order.

Why are they procrastinating to begin with?

For starters, procrastination is part of human nature. It is much easier to sit on the couch than it is to get up and paint the fence.By the same token, they have been doing fine (at least in their eyes) up until now without our product, why should they be in a hurry to sign on the dotted line with us before they've "gotten all their ducks in a row"?

If they are still stagnant after we have presented and followed up properly, there is nothing wrong with pointing out the elephant in the room.Ask them why they aren't moving forward?They took the appointment, made the inquiry, or requested the estimate because they were interested in buying right?

What haven't YOU done to ensure they are ready to move forward? Ask yourself this, but equally important, ask the customer the same question.Eight out of ten times, one of you will have the answer here.Perhaps they don't see the value yet. . . show them.Maybe you haven't explained pricing properly. . .show them.It's possible they feel the need to shop around still.If this is the case, resist the urge to besmirch your competition.Instead, build yourself and your product up by selling each benefit your product offers and your competition can't (the customer should come to their own conclusions without you blatantly hammering the point).

Now, no matter whether you feel it's time or not, toss in a simple "why don't we go ahead and get this off your to-do list" close.You'll be surprised at how often this will work. At the very least, it will bring out an objection beyond "OK... I have your number, I'm gonna chew on this.".

Point number two above, brings up a strange phenomenon that has only grown more prevalent in the information age.

Our customers often feel as if they've done the research, they just want to buy without being sold. Here's where we straddle the razor's edge.We have to figure out how to show them the benefits without outright selling.

One might think an educated client is a good thing right?An

educated client is indeed, great, however it is important to remember how they received that education.More than likely, they have performed Google-Fu and now feel that their grasp of product knowledge and pricing is on par with yours.They know how your competitors are priced and sadly, are probably expecting to get the bait-and-switch price advertised online for nearly every product imaginable.

Rather than play salesperson/customer, why not team up with a client like this? They've shown enough interest and initiative to learn about what we do and how we do it.Why not merely peel back the curtain and let them sell themselves?Their inclusion in the process gains ultimate buy-in and how can they object with themselves.This also throws price out the window.

A perfect example of the above statement is these "Build Your Own Burger" restaurants. Sure, for $8.99 you can order the pre-designed Ranch Hand Burger w/ fries.You can also use this tiny golf pencil and run down our list of ingredients to build your perfect burger.The secret is, that burger YOU designed, has a way higher profit margin because you either tossed enough crap on there to run the price up to $11.99 or you skimped so hard that your $9.99 build-a-burger cost less to make than ordering one of the pre-designed burgers sans an ingredient or two.Either way, customer and restaurant are happy!

Finally, by painting the vision of what their life will look and feel like post-purchase, we can set them in motion.

The truth is if the customer is procrastinating now, they will continue to do so.It is our job to show them this reality.

First, weave the tale of the extra time and energy they will spend by shopping around or the money they will lose each day/week/month by not moving forward.Remind them of the guy who drives to five different stores to buy a washer and dryer, only to finally end up returning to the first store after wasting his entire Sunday and missing the game.

Next, paint the picture of how good it will feel to have this task completed.They can cross it off their list and move on with their lives.Waiting to buy only means that feeling of completion will be delayed further and they'll have to deal with more salespeople that might not be as personable as you.

# HOMEWORK

WARNING!

This homework assignment requires some self-awareness.

I want you to reflect on the last year of your life.

What is the one thing you procrastinated the most? For me, it was actually writing the first book in this series. I started writing with a fury and promptly set it all aside for THREE MONTHS while I dreamt of how cool it would be to publish a book (all the while, not working toward publishing a book).

Did you ever complete the task or are you still putting it off?

Why did you put it off to begin with?

What stood in your way of completion?

If you did complete the task/project, what motivated you to finally finish?

We talk all the time about being empathetic with our clients. Understanding why they procrastinate these major decisions and hamper our ability to close the deal is important. Without understanding the problem, it is impossible to find the solution.

Understanding that we are also human and human nature is to procrastinate will allow us to get inside the prospective customer's head and get them on the path to action.

# ICE CREAM!

Ever yell "FIRE!" in a movie theater? Please don't try it. There's a reason why it is illegal. Imagine though, how frantically fast people would be climbing over each other to get out of that place.

Now think back about how fast you moved when you heard the faintest tinkling of the ice cream truck's music as a child. You ran or pedaled home, burst through the door, begged for money from your parents, ran back out and ran or pedaled in the general direction of that jingle like a bat out of hell.

Both examples get folks moving quickly. The truth is though, as humans, we run faster from pain than we do toward pleasure. It makes sense. You'd certainly move faster to save your life than to get an Eskimo pie. Even on a hot day!

Apply this to your day to day in sales. Are you giving people reason to want to work with you?

It is all too easy to fall into the opposite track. The call or meeting doesn't start the way we want it, and we start getting a little negative. Our customer picks up on it and they start to close off. Often times, this is right where we lose the sale.

How about this one? We toss in a close and they give us a bullshit smokescreen of an objection. Rather than calmly dealing with it, we get snarky. Chalk up another loss.

The hits keep on coming right? We follow up with a prospect.

They act like they are too busy to take the call and blow us off. Our knee-jerk reaction is to be a full jerk and voila! Another prospective sale down the drain.

Do any of these sound familiar to you?

If you have read book one in this series, followed my blog, listened to my podcast or followed me on Twitter, you know what I am about to say. It's time to get out of your own way!

Why do we do this to ourselves?

It's crazy. We put in all the work. We prospect for a lead. We fight for the appointment. We prepare for the appointment. We take the time to primp for the appointment; I even count drive time and dry cleaning in this. Then, when it matters the most, we give in to that little devil on our shoulder and yell "FIRE!". All that prep work, time, energy, even money are out the window. All because we gave in to our base instincts and let adrenalin get the best of us.

How many times have you heard "take a deep breath" in your lifetime? You've heard it because it works. That long, cleansing breath works wonders. The forced three count of a deep breath not only calms the nerves, but it also gives your brain time to take over.

I mean that. When our nerves and adrenalin kick in, we go on autopilot. We say and do things that we don't really mean and often end up regretting. I said it a few sentences above. It's time we got out of our own way.

Let's look at the examples above. We start our sales presentation and can tell our prospect is distracted. Rather than get pissed off and say something snide, why not politely address the elephant in the room. We don't know what crisis may have hit them right beforehand. Why not ask them if they need to take a minute or two? "Y'know what Jon, I can tell you are a little distracted. Do you need a minute to catch your breath before we continue? I can shave a few minutes off this presentation if I cut out the jokes." If they truly were in distress, they will thank you for the consideration. If they DON'T need the time, you better believe you will have their undivided from there on out.

Remember, we cannot control what goes on outside of our bubble. We never know what our customers are doing or saying five minutes before we arrive. Have they gotten bad news? Have they gotten amazing news? Are they missing an important deadline by taking this meeting? If they are too distracted, you won't make the sale right then and there anyway. Give them the opportunity to regroup. It will be in your favor bank.

The root cause here is not your fault. How you respond to it is.

In the second example, we are totally to blame. Go into every sales call expecting to get objections. We are not selling until we hit that first objection anyway. It's manna when we do get those sales without objections, but in that situation, you are just an order taker. The freebies only count in metrics.

So the client gives us a smokescreen. Don't get angry. Remember, here is where the sale starts! Acknowledge it and respond to it relevantly. Deal with their objection, no matter how big or how small and close again. Don't get emotional. Don't grip the bat too tight. Just deal with it and close.

If the objections are still there, retreat and regroup. Pushing harder at that point either turns you into the "pushy used car salesman" or worse, makes you sound desperate. Sometimes, the objection we here is just there as a defense mechanism to hold us at bay because the customer has something else to deal with that has nothing to do with us or this transaction. Whether we push them too hard or we pull back, the end result of this conversation/meeting will be the same. One option affords you the opportunity to come back later and try again, while the other burns the bridge.

The third scenario above is another one that is up to us. We have no idea what is going on in a customer's life when we get them on the phone. Are they in line at the grocery? Are they taking a dump? Are they fighting with their spouse? Did they answer by accident thinking it was the doctor calling in with test results? All of these are very real occurrences that happen every day. We must be mindful and empathetic.

Just like the example above, consider the potential outcomes. If we shoot back at them and put some stank on it, what good can come of it. We will get that temporary rush of "I told them!" then immediately feel regret. Fuck first impressions, you don't get a second chance to make any impressions, so don't be that guy (or girl).

If we cause our clients pain on the phone or during a presentation, what are the chances they will let us back into their lives? Pretty slim. The next time you call, you will be swiped right to ignoresville.

So, the next time your inner asshole wants to come out, keep in mind that people run toward the ice cream man. People love the ice cream man.

# HOMEWORK

You catch more flies with sugar than with vinegar.

For this assignment, I want you to come up with ten ways to handle negative situations.

For example, muting your phone (silence is important here) and taking a deep, cleansing breath when a customer gets nasty with you. Yes, MUTE THE DAMN PHONE when you do this. Letting them hear a giant sigh is just as bad taking a negative tone.

One example that one of my favorite sales leaders gave us long ago was to end all calls by saying "Thank you for your time". It is amazing how many rough edges that statement smooths over. Customers will forgive many minor transgressions when they hear that to end a call.

If you need help with this, I recommend reading a summary or cliff notes of "How To Win Friends And Influence People" by Dale Carnegie. This is the consummate book on people skills. It's quite a long read, so I condone the synopsis for brevity's sake.

# THICKEN YOUR SKIN

A burned bridge won't rebuild itself. Standing there and staring won't get you to the other side. Why as salespeople, do we act as if this will work?

Does this scenario sound familiar to you? We put in a ton of time and energy with a prospect. They string us along for weeks, only to ultimately leave us for their barber's referral solely on price. To add insult to injury, they end up using the exact program you customized for them. This leech came in last minute and didn't even do any work. All they did was plug in your work and give the cut-rate price.

How fucking pissed off are you when this happens? Here's a nice nut punch for a cherry on top. You don't want to hear this, but you have no one to blame but yourself. I promised you when we started working together that I'm not going to sugar coat things.

Here's the reality. You created this particular monster. They didn't need all that time to make their decision. You gave them that time. Had you done the work up front and closed sooner, they'd be happily working with you.

What? You say they weren't ready to move forward yet? That's on you too. Did you properly gauge their interest level and timeline? What was your follow-up game like? If they were discussing this with their barber, they clearly had interest. When was the last time you spoke with them?

If you were following up, what was your game plan? Chances are, you were phoning it in with the "Just checking in" call and offered up one or two yes or no questions before they shut you down with "Well, I've got your number.". I don't want to get off track too much on follow-up here, because I have entire chapters and podcast episodes devoted to this, but live by the mantra "If it is worth doing, it is worth doing right." Don't sell yourself short on follow-ups. Your prospects will take you as seriously as you take yourself.

If you are checking in like a telemarketer, that is how you will be perceived. Would you want your financial planner to be a lion or a lamb? It doesn't matter what you are selling, if you don't exude confidence, you won't find success. They say "Dress for the job you want", "Fake it 'til you make it", and "Act as if" for a reason. They are all sound pieces of advice!

Back to our client who dumped us. I think I've done a decent job of putting the blame back on you. What can we do about it? Assuming that ship has sailed, we have to learn to let go. Negativity breeds negativity. Learn from your mistakes and move on. Dwelling on it does no good. We won't win them back over by blowing up their phone. Getting more pissed off about it will affect how you deal with your next prospects as well. Shake it off and move on.

There is a reason that so few sports teams in history have ever gone undefeated. You truly cannot win them all, but you can learn from them all. Whether it's a victory or a loss, there is something to be learned from every at bat.

When we let the losses follow us around, it shows. We wear it on our faces. We wear it in our attitude. Our customers can hear it, smell it, even taste it. Going into your sales presentation like this is straight up bush league. You'd be better off canceling or postponing the meeting. Your net result will be the same. Take the day off and regroup.

Let's look at how this can affect you on a micro scale now.

How familiar does this one sound? We are on a warm call. These folks at least expressed interest in our product in some way, yet they cut us off at the pass and legit disrespect us like we're some offshore IRS scam call. We can't get a word in edge-wise and our adrenalin rush hits like an EMP.

This is just like those stats "Every minute in the US, a car accident occurs". Calls like this happen every day, every hour, and every minute on sales floors around the world. Like Tyler Durden says "You are not a unique snowflake". Get over it. What good can dwelling on this do?

Sit back and look at your options here:

1. Calling them back will only escalate the situation. End result, more anger and no sale. It could possibly end in unemployment as well.

2. We can break shit. This feels good temporarily, but a few minutes later, we will be embarrassed, regretful and have to replace what we broke, so our net is a negative cash flow.

3. We can bitch and moan to our co-workers. What is the end game here? We will bring them down too. Would we want them to do the same to us? You better be sure they will eventually return the favor and instantly cool your hot hand next time. Picture a half-dozen or so willing participants on the average sales floor and you can see this sales cancer spreading pretty quickly

can't you?

4. We can let it go. We've established that shit happens. People are people. Letting it go means you have a better shot at making the next sale.

As you can see, only one option really leads to success here. Even if you can come up with fifty more possible actions, the outcomes are the same. You have to learn to let it go.

I know this is all easier said than done. We all fall prey to these traps. It is human nature. Remember, the average human cannot sell like you do. You have an ability that mere mortals don't necessarily possess. Knowing this, you can't be surprised when success requires you to do things beyond human nature and rise above instinct.

Getting out of your own way requires thoughtfulness empathy, and mindfulness.

# HOMEWORK

This chapter's homework has nothing to do with sales... and everything to do with sales.

I want you to go out and join a gym. If you belong to a gym, I want you to actually go to that gym. If you already go to that gym regularly, I want you to email me and tell me your secret to gym consistency.

No, this is not so you can take notes on the gym's sales tactics. I just want you to work out.

Get the urge to break stuff when a client pisses you off? Join a gym with a heavy bag and beat the shit out of it.

Have trouble letting go of your stress? Join a yoga studio and get lost in yourself.

Whatever type of gym you join, use it as an escape. Put on headphones, listen to your jams, an audio book, or The Seven Minute Sales Minute Podcast. Just get lost for an hour in yourself. Your body will thank you for keeping in shape and your mind will thank you too.

# AVATARS ARE NOT ALL BLUE

Customer Avatar. This overused buzzword is thrown around all over the place these days, but what is it? Why do guru-preneurs in all fields toss the term around so much?

In simplest terms, your customer avatar is merely your ideal target market. Using the buzzword just sounds cooler.

In a previous chapter, I write about "being the ice cream man". Let's look a little bit at how the ice cream man might define his customer avatar.

First, if he is geographically in an area with clearly defined seasons, he probably is best working between March and September. Other areas might afford him a better opportunity to work more months out of the year, so if he is not tied to a specific location, this can be adjusted for. Knowing right off the bat that his ideal times to do business might be limited, he may want to look into other seasonal businesses or even a seasonal location.

Next, what is his ideal customer age and gender? Ice cream knows no boundaries when it comes to gender, so in this respect he wins. Everyone likes his product equally. Age-wise, I would operate under the assumption that his ideal avatar would be kids of school age. Where do we find such clientele?

Between March and June, it seems obvious that during school hours, he can kick his feet up. Once the school bells start to ring, he should be out and about playing his music for all to hear. Once school is out for the year, all bets are off. His workday can begin at lunchtime and run through sundown.

Now... if I was the ice cream man, I would be a little more devious. Knowing that I have downtime during the day, I would seek out a shopping center or two that had a gym or yoga studio, a Weight Watchers and health food store and troll the neighborhoods surrounding it with my music turned up super loud. I would also stock some "healthy" alternatives such as frozen yogurt and other "diet" ice creams. Who better to supplement my income than someone we already know is battling the bulge and has just worked up an appetite or just gotten news (good or bad) at their weigh-in? I don't mind being an ice cream enabler. It's not like we are selling drugs now is it?

The ice cream man is a very simple business that allows for simple generalizations when it comes to defining your avatar. As you define down your ideal customer, it is ok to get more granular. The more you know about your prospects, the better prepared you can be.

By being better prepared we will dramatically improve our odds of making the sale.

Knowing our market makes this prep that much easier.

Let's define our market:

1. Our Customer Avatar

What is the age of your target client? Sex? Marital status? Education level? Are they employed? If so, what line of work are they in? What is their average household income?

Do these questions sound familiar? Chances are, you've answered them countless times in surveys over the years. This information is invaluable as you begin to target your marketing and sales pitch.

2. Know your competition

Your customers are not loyal until you give them a reason to be. By the time you have had a chance to pitch your product or service, they've definitely done some research on you and your competition. If they haven't yet, they will. This is not a negative. You do the same thing when you are looking to buy something. We live in the information age. It's all too easy to get information (and misinformation) about any topic.

I want to know as much about my competition as they can. What do they do well? What do they do poorly? How is their product similar to my product and how are they different? How can I best exploit their weaknesses and downplay their strengths?

Take cellphone providers for instance. It has long been a given that here in the US, Verizon offers the most rock solid performance as a network. They have also been cemented as the most expensive carrier around. By contrast, in most areas of the country, Sprint is known for nearly polar opposite reasons. Their plans and pricing have been known to be much less expensive and have less strict credit requirements, while network reliability may be less reliable.

It is easy to resort to mudslinging in order to make your point and differentiate yourself here, but how can we do it without shining too much light on the competition?

If I work for Verizon, I am painting the vision of luxury and evoking imagery of Mercedes Benz, Rolex and Apple. These are products that just work. You know that when you turn the key or power them up, you can count on them to work. You want to know that should you be lost in the middle of nowhere, your phone will have a signal and you will find your way home safely. You want to know that when your child has an emergency, they'll be able to contact you instantly and effortlessly. Sure, the service might cost you an extra $20 a month, but isn't that a small price to pay to know your family is safe and secure? This is pretty much how I have seen it played every time I have dealt with them.

On the Sprint side, I would play it almost exactly as they have in their current marketing. They are highlighting the marked improvement in their network while not increasing cost to do so. Showing the overall percentage of drop calls vs. the competition and highlighting the disproportionate price vs. quality differences is a great way to show that you lose very little in the overall benefits of the product for the large savings you enjoy.

I say I'd play it *almost* exactly the same as Sprint has because I would change one major thing. I would not have hired the ex-Verizon spokesman to be my pitchman. Sloppy seconds are just plain sloppy.

Both examples above make good use of the strengths of each company against the weaknesses of the other without resorting to trash talking the competition. Remember, we get higher by elevating ourselves than by knocking others down.

I am sure you can weigh-in on your own cellphone provider pitches as well. That's exactly why I use them as an example. That is exactly why I chose this to illustrate the point.

Knowing your market

By clearly defining our target market and knowing our competition, we will be infinitely more prepared for our sales presentations and possible objections thrown our way. We'll know what other options our prospects are seeing in the market as they shop and we'll know how to counteract the strengths of our competition while minimizing our own weaknesses.

# HOMEWORK

Hopefully, this one comes easy to you because you should have been thinking about this while reading the chapter.

What is your avatar?

List ten attributes that define your perfect client.

Now break down each item on that list. What problem are we solving for that particular line item?

Does our prospective client know they have this problem? If not, how do we bring it to their attention so we can solve it?

If our client is aware that they have this problem, are they aware we have the solution? If not, how can we make them aware?

If they already know we can solve the problem, how can we convince them that the problem needs to be solved today and we are just the ones to solve it for them?

Just like the Ice Cream Man hanging outside Weight Watchers, I want you to repeat this process for a secondary and tertiary avatar. You may have a perfect customer in your head, but your product certainly was created for more than just a narrow slice of the world. By repeating this process, we can find ways to tailor our sales presentations to many different demographics. Having this knowledge is invaluable.

# ASSUMPTION GUMPTION

This one always throws newer salespeople off.

From a young age, we are taught, "When you assume, you make an ASS out of U and ME". Then in sales trainings around the world, we are told that we should always be assumptive.

Wait...? What? I should be skinny and fat? I should be tall and short. I should be sorry/not sorry?

Yes... you should be assumptive and non-assumptive at the same time. Just do them for different reasons.

There is never a reason in sales to not be assumptive. You should always assume the sale. Act as if my brothers and sisters!

I have written blog posts about assuming the sale. I have done podcasts about being assumptive. In my day job, I have inherited an amazing training on this very topic that has evolved 30 Minute Sales Coach style into something our newer sales-folk remember forever.

We will go into the power of being assumptive at a later date.

Today, we are going to talk about the *weakness* of being assumptive. Yeah, I told you this one might be a little out there.

So if we are supposed to be assumptive, why are you telling us not to be assumptive?

It's simple. As humans, we tend to fill in the blanks on unknown variables in order to shape our own narrative. We jump to conclusions. We build monuments to nothing. We get angry. We get sad. We think the worst. We do a lot of dumb shit that doesn't need to get done.

See? It turns out the ass making statements we grew up with were right after all. Being assumptive at the wrong time can wreak havoc on our business and mindset.

I have seen this all too many times. We prejudge the hell out of a prospect. "It's a single mom, she can't afford it.", "That guy is from (insert country here). I know exactly how this will play out." The hits go on and on. They say don't judge a book by its cover, yet we (we are all guilty of it at some point) still allow our subconscious to talk us out of a sale.

While we're talking about judging books by their covers, here's one for you. A friend of mine sells high-end automobiles. He's great at what he does. He knows the cars inside and out and has mastered the art of suggesting how much of a stud you look like behind the wheel without going too far. He has seen tons of salespeople come and go at his dealership while he has consistently built up a book of business on past clients and referrals.

If you ask him his secret, it won't be what you expect. The secret to his success is not judging people when they walk into the showroom. The world of luxury vehicle sales is a little topsy-turvy. Prejudge the wrong person as a tire-kicker and you kiss thousands goodbye and can ruin a long-lasting relationship before it even starts.

The folks who don't make it in his line of work assume the wrong thing.

"That punk kid who walked onto the lot? He'll never buy, he's just here to waste my time." What you don't know is that he's got a trust fund that dwarves your net worth. Or maybe he is shopping for his father, who is too buys making millions to come in and pick out his own car. Perhaps he just signed a record deal. You just lost a sale.

"Look at what that guy is wearing. I bet one of my shoes cost more than his wardrobe." Ever think that he likes cars more than clothes or maybe he just sold his software company for a few mil and has been locked away in front of his keyboard for months? You just lost another sale.

I could go on and on, the stereotypes and archetypes are endless and the more I type, the less PC I'll get.

The one person my friend will never make a beeline for is the guy who comes in dressed to the nines. You know the one. Four figure suit over Ferragamos fidgeting just enough so you can see his beefy Panerai. That's the guy who is probably NOT going to buy. This is usually the guy who dressed the part looking for a free joy ride.

The people who can afford to buy a six-figure automobile are confident enough to know they are able to afford it without trying to prove it to you. The ones that come in wearing jeans and flip-flops end up being the best repeat customers. The Ferragamo-fidgeters are the ones who either don't buy or freak out about their first oil-change invoice.

These examples may be a little elementary, but they serve to prove a point. When we prejudge our clients and let our subconscious make assumptions about who/what they are, we are leaving business on the table.

Coming from a phone sales background, I have learned firsthand as both the direct sales person and coach, the importance of not assuming anything about clients on the phone. There are quite a few reasons, but here are a few samples.

1. You don't know what they were doing when that phone rang, so their behavior on that particular call may not be indicative of who they are.

2. Accent doesn't equate to IQ. I know guys from the south who exploit this to the fullest. They just know (are they assuming too?) that when they get a Yankee on the line, they are being underestimated.

3. We have no idea what the prospect was expecting if they called in to us. Were they expecting to just briefly set an appointment for a later conversation when we talked their ear off for forty minutes?

4. We don't know who else is in the room with them. Are they being guarded because they are in a cubicle farm and don't want to share their personal info in public?

5. Why are they calling us? They might sound like they really have their act together, so we think they want product A and take that path. Had we dug a little deeper, we may realize they need real help and plan B or C is the better choice.

In the end, there are so many opportunities for us to mess this up every day. Every industry will have their own unique pitfalls to look out for. We must be cognizant of this at all times and assume nothing.

Treat your clients as if this is your first day on the planet and they are fascinating to you. Learn what problem they want/need to solve and show them how you can provide the solution in a way that no one else can. We are here to serve our clients and in return get compensated for it. We are not here to judge them.

Remember, the guy in flip-flops with socks doesn't walk into the Ferrari dealership without good reason.

# HOMEWORK

This assignment is another one of those more "esoteric" ones.

I want you to go into every conversation in your life (sales or otherwise) with a completely open mind for the next seven days.

This won't be easy. As humans, we tend to pre-judge on almost a minute-by-minute basis.

Any time you feel yourself assuming something about another person, you must fight the urge and accept that we are all beings with free will and you cannot accurately predict anyone else's thoughts, emotions or actions.

Of all the crazy homework assignments I have given in these books so far, this one will definitely be one of the hardest. If you complete it fully and take it seriously though, I promise it will pay huge dividends.

By not assuming anything about your customers, you will be freed of the burden of acting based on actions they never actually do and statements they never actually make. You will be free to act in the moment and react to their true feelings.

Your customers will sense this and they will feel how you are genuinely in the moment with them. This translates into more business and ultimately way more referrals because folks will want to share their experience with others.

# FINAL THOUGHTS

Over the last 14 months, I have had the opportunity to share more of myself with others than ever before. Between the podcast and my first book, the response has been overwhelming. I relish the positive feedback and am encouraged every day by those who share their successes with me.

Hell, I even love the occasional trollish comment or email about the show or book. You are free to like or dislike the work I put out there.

In the end, I do this for you, the reader, the listener the protege. I want nothing more than to see you succeed. When I am able to solve a particular problem you are having or role-play out a difficult sale, it invigorates me.

I promised when this started to make myself available to you. Some folks have taken me up on it and found success. I encourage you to reach out to me if you are looking for answers. I'm not selling any crazy webinars or thousand dollar an hour consulting gigs. I have mentored hundreds of folks over the years. Take advantage. Visit me at www.30MinuteSalesCoach.com anytime and reach out.

# THE 30 MINUTE SALES COACH PRESENTS...

**Sell Smartest**

Optimize Your Mindset For Sales Success

*You inspire me to grow every day. I could not ask for a more perfect daughter.*

# ALL FOR YOU

It has been a crazy few months since launching the first 30 Minute Sales Coach book.

I have gotten great feedback and reviews and also have taken some solid criticism. All of it is helpful and wholly appreciated.

One thing I know for sure is that people are getting their money's worth out of these books and then some. I am providing insight collected over twenty plus years in sales and it is paying off in spades for many of you out there. This makes me smile more than anything else.

You will notice in book three that I am foregoing the homework model. At this point, if you've read book one and two and done your homework, you are ready for book three's mental checkups. If you haven't read book one and two, go back and do so after enjoying this third installment.

There is a lot of mindset and psychology in this part of the series. The first two books are meant to get you thinking more about your business, your prospects and your actual customers.

This book is meant to give a higher level overview of your business and tips on improving.

There is not a salesperson out there that hasn't struggled from time to time. Even when we are at the top of our game we still suffer from self-doubt half the time by nature.

I want you to always be able to reach up to your shelf or your phone, tablet or kindle and get something from my books. It might be a kick in the pants. Sometimes, it's an ego fluff. You might just need a little tip or trick to tweak your game. Sometimes, just a reminder that you are not alone out there. What's important is that you gain something from the small investment you made in buying my books.

Much of what you will find in here comes directly from conversations with many of you. You spoke and I listened. You emailed and I read. Some of you tweeted and it went down in the DM.

It probably sounds like hokey bullshit, but I really did write these books for you. I'm not swimming like Scrooge McDuck in Kindle money over here. This is info I wanted and needed to share, so I did. I want you to do something with it. Earn more money. Live better. Have less stress. I hope you take a ton away from me. Please, if you do, share it. My email is still scott@30MinuteSalesCoach.com and I love hearing from you guys and gals.

# YOU HAVE SPOKEN

You, the readers, have spoken.

I've asked in my books, newsletters, and countless tweets for you to bring me your questions, comments, and feedback. You did not disappoint.

Sell Smartest is mainly comprised of chapters that came out of these conversations and requests.

It amazes me that there are so many books and courses designed to teach you the mechanics of the sales process, but so few geared toward the psychology behind sales and the mindset of the salespeople themselves.

In the pages that follow most of the chapters have come directly from conversations with you.

I say it over and over again: we are in this together. I am not Ben Affleck in Boiler Room throwing Ferrari keys on the table. That's not how I roll. Plus, everyone knows my car, motorcycle, and other car are BMW Maybe I should trade them all in for a Ferrari. Not sure what I'd drive in these Michigan winters though.

We truly are in the trenches together each and every day. Yes, I am still coaching and mentoring, but when the dust settles, I make my bones on the phones. I am prospecting, interviewing and pitching all day every day.

What works for you will work for me and vice-versa because we are one and the same. I am not coming to you from my fake-ass ivory tower offering you some bad infomercial webinar about how to get rich in sales. I am here to help you actually sell to actual real clients in the real world.

I am taking my lumps alongside you. I share my wins. I share my losses. I am human. Hear me roar!

# OBSTACLE COURSE

What is your biggest obstacle in sales?

I have been coaching salespeople for nearly two decades, and each of us has our own speed bumps and roadblocks that impede or even stop us from succeeding.

Sometimes, these impediments are very real. Most of the time however, we create these blockages in our own heads. We are human. Humans are very good at rationalizing. It's also human nature to deflect blame. We are the hero of our story, so how on earth can the hero be failing. Something else must be causing this.

It has been a recurring theme in my books and I expect it will continue to be so, but the SECOND place you should look is right in the mirror.

I say this is the second place you should look because it is extremely important to first lay some blame. What is the knee jerk obstacle to your success? I mean really, when someone says "why do you suck?", what is the first reason that comes to mind? Where is that initial finger pointing directed?

Now take this reason you came up with and write it down on a blank sheet of paper. Stare at it. Get to know it.

Next, write down all the reasons how this is stopping you from finding success.

Next, write down all the reasons why this is hindering you.

Lastly, write down all the reasons when this occurs.

This is your super villain. This is the one thing we must overcome to find sales success.

Our next step is a little tough. It requires some serious emotional intelligence.

Let's diagnose the how. If this is stopping you from making sales, how can you avoid this? Now, hit the why and the when.

By completing this exercise, nine times out of ten, you will realize that the reason you think you are not succeeding is often not the reason at all. You will find that what you need to succeed lies within you.

If what we need to find success is located inside of us, I would bet that the entire reason you are NOT succeeding also lies inside of you. At this point, I would hope that you have already read two of my books, so you should be ready for this statement: It is time to get out of your own way.

Stop projecting. Stop blaming. Stop being a victim. Stop inviting failure. All of these are mindset killers and do you no good.

If you believe you will fail, you will fail.

There are enough real distractions and obstacles in this world. The sooner you stop contributing to the detrimental clutter, the better off you will be. Choose success.

# TEACH & LEARN

Those who can't do, teach.

We've talked about this before. A generalization like this is bad. Can all who teach also perform at a high level? Probably not. Can all who perform at a high level also teach people how to replicate their success? Also a big probably not. To make a blanket statement like this is bad.

I have learned something very valuable over the years about teaching. This simple fact can be a career changer when you take it to heart. Everybody should teach from time to time.

Something miraculous happens when you are able to explain something to someone less experienced than you are. You gain a new confidence in your own knowledge and abilities that may not have previously been there. This confidence pays off tenfold in solidifying the foundation of your career.

Working as a sales leader, I leveraged the shit out of this. What's funny is that my protégés often thought I was just delegating to delegate and shirking my responsibilities. It wasn't until they were with me for a while that they realized I was truly teaching them much more just by having them "do my job". If someone in their third month was assigned to help someone in month one learn a specific task, they had this fresh in their head. They also had their finger on the pulse of what is going on "in the weeds" every day rather than a higher level managerial view.

What is great about this is as the month three associate teaches, their own understanding of the material is solidified, corroborated, and cemented. They are able to strut their stuff and have a little swagger knowing that they have a grasp on this good enough to warrant teaching it.

Of course, I was always there to supervise and watch from afar to ensure things were being taught properly. I was never as hands off as I portrayed. I still had to sign off on everyone's ability, so I would step in where needed.

In this respect, I challenge everyone out there to try their hands at teaching every once in awhile. You have to really work to master something in order to teach it properly. Just as you had to master a topic in school in order to give a speech or write a paper on it.

If you are in sales management/leadership and you are trying to control everything without delegating, I challenge you to let go. By giving some of your employees' autonomy to master and teach a topic, you free yourself up to learn more skills that you in turn can master and teach to your charges.

With this cycle of expanded knowledge and skill, you can ensure that you will constantly be improving and moving in the right direction.

Strive to master every topic enough to be able to teach it. If you can teach a less seasoned salesperson, you sure as hell can teach a client. Teach your clients and they will forever be indebted to you. No one likes feeling lost and at the mercy of their salesperson. It makes them uneasy and less likely to buy.

A bush league sales guy will want to keep his prospects off balance and lord his expertise over them. A confident and knowledgeable salesperson will educate his/her client in order to lead them to a comfortable decision.

A tree is either growing or dying. Seeking knowledge guarantees that you stay on the growth path longer. The more you grow and more knowledge you gather, the more relevant and valuable you stay.

# BE THEIR "GUY"

Who is the person in your group of friends who everyone calls when they "need a guy"? You know, no matter what you need done, "he's got a guy" and sends you over there with a "tell 'em I sent ya."

Maybe you are the guy. Since you are in sales, there is a good chance you are. How can you ensure that your clients think of you as "their guy" to refer their friends and family to?

One way to get them to at least think about it is to do a great job and treat them well. By showing them you've got the stuff, they surely will shout your name from the rooftops, right?

Well... what if they don't?

Maybe, just maybe, they really aren't sure if you want or accept referrals. How did they find you? Were they referred? Or were they a generated lead?

Not only do we have to make sure that our clients and prospects know that we accept referrals, we have to let them know we want and even expect them.

You should be asking for or at least bringing up referrals every time you speak to a prospect or client.

Wait? We haven't earned the right yet! You earned the right the second you committed to helping them. Even during the very first conversation "I plan to wow you so much that you can't wait to send friends and family my way so I can help them too."

This is a great foreshadow and it opens the door for future requests.

Ending the fact finding initial interview. "Who else do you know that I can help out?".

How about this one. Rather than waiting until after the deal is signed, sealed, and delivered, strike when they are basking in the glow of saying yes. This just might be their happiest point. You never know what stresses they will go through as you handle paperwork and due diligence prior to consummation. When they say yes, they are happy and confident in their decision and are in lockstep with you.

The one time I usually avoid the referral ask is signing day. At this point, they are probably a little overwhelmed and may even have a little tinge of buyer's remorse. They may be thinking back to some information and paperwork requests from your support staff or pushback from members of their organization.

I usually check in later that day to make sure all went smoothly and let them know I will follow up. This allows me to take their temperature on how the transaction closed in their perception.

This allows me to plan my attack. If all went well, I know they are basking in that glow and I can ask the very next day. I might even hit them with the email including five numbered spaces asking for folks that could use my assistance.

If they are still a little salty, I provide the normal follow up and excellent service over the next week and make sure all rough edges and ruffled feathers are smoothed. Depending on compliance for your business, a token thank you gift works wonders here as well. Then, once I have reminded them of my worth, I then ask for referrals.

Remember, people don't always think about referring your business. It is not their job to ensure you put food on your table. You are the captain of that particular ship, so you must make sure you let them know you expect to exceed their expectations enough so that they cannot help but send you friends, family, coworkers, etc… You have to ask.

# OUTCOME FOCUSED

When working toward a sale, it is important that you keep the proper objective in focus. If I am not mistaken, our sole mission is to make the sale. The customer gets the new product and we get a new client and hopefully some referrals out of the deal.

In any war with one's salt, there is more than one battle to be fought. We must remember that we should only fight the battles that have us moving toward our goals of closing the deal. Don't let emotions get the best of you and get dragged into inconsequential battles that get you nowhere (or even put you further back).

Our prospects don't know our product or process as well as we do, so they will want to do whatever they can to gain some ground and win a battle here and there. This means you need to be ready for them to pick some "fights" that can derail the conversation. They might bring up price, your competition, your reputation, their past experiences, etc... This is a natural defense and not something they are always doing purposefully.

The prospect will often have concerns in their head based on preconceived notions that may or may not be true. Some of these concerns might have been built up into full blown "issues" in their heads as they created their mental vision of you and your product before the meeting.

It is fine to acknowledge these and if they are relevant let them know you will address their concerns in a moment. Not only is it fine to acknowledge these, you have to. You can't let them feel ignored, but you also shouldn't let them take the meeting over based on straw arguments. Remember, they don't know the product yet, so many of their concerns may be unfounded and not based in reality.

While you are continuing the conversation, you can even slyly address their concerns while working your way through your sales process without actually calling attention to it. In this way, they will know that their initial concern was valid, but unnecessary.

Knowing full well that there will be more important battles ahead, I will sometimes even concede a small one here or there as they come up. Letting the client know they are right and acknowledging the "win" goes a long way in humanizing you and also cushioning the blow when future battles are not in their favor.

Letting them win is strategic and will allow you to keep moving without losing too much momentum. There is no shame in taking an L here or there. No one goes undefeated. You just need to make sure that you win when it counts.

Remember, you are behind the wheel. Keep things moving forward. Don't get sidetracked on minutiae that gets you nowhere. Let them take a potty break here and there, but you don't need to take the off-ramp for every exit with a Waffle House.

# THE CONVERSATIONALIST

Why do we feel the need to suck the air out of the room on a sales call?

For many sales professionals, we keep talking to fill the empty space because we are either uncomfortable or we are trying to distract and deflect our prospect.

A good sales presentation should be a conversation, not an infomercial or interrogation.

This is one that is not always our fault (I know, right? Scott isn't blaming us for once.). Our prospects often hit us like a tornado with a deluge of questions that are semi-relevant to what they actually want. And we have to be the experts steering them in the right direction.

This is understandable. They come to us worried more about the bottom line and protecting themselves from getting ripped off than what the value and benefit of our product is. They don't know what to ask, so they default to price.

It is our job to get them talking. The old standby of disarming them with humor can really work wonders. Get them to chuckle and you have won half the battle. Now you just need to get them to open up one question at a time.

Make sure your questions have relevance. Remember, they are not our friends at this point, so they are still approaching us as if we are a strange dog. Any sudden move could possibly scare them away.

Peel away those layers one by one until you get to the core of why you are talking in the first place and show them why they need you and your product.

Approach your sales presentations and interviews in this manner, and you will not only cultivate new business, but you will create referral sources. Approach your prospects like everyone else does and you will be lumped into the same category as them. The sales guy who needs to give them a "deal" to get them on board.

Having good conversations builds the like, trust, and respect pyramid equally in all directions. Keep it up and you will have clients for life.

# THINK LIKE AN OWNER

When you work in a sales position, you work for someone else, be it a small company or large corporation. Make no mistake though. You also work for YOU.

The second you stop acting like an employee and start acting like a business owner, things change. No longer will you be quick to cut margins to close a sale. No longer will you show up at the opening bell without proper prep for the day. You will pay closer attention at meetings. You will command more respect from your clients because you will have the air of ownership.

When you think like an owner, you come to the table with a solution rather than telling your superiors you have a problem.

Along those lines, you start to think of folks as your leaders, and no longer your superiors.

Your desk or office is YOUR lemonade stand. You have parameters and boundaries you need to operate within, but you are the master of this particular domain.

This is one of my favorite aspects of working in sales. Yes, I answer to my leaders. But if I am hitting numbers, what can they really say when I bounce at 3 on a Wednesday to hit the gym? Along those lines, as an owner, I have absolutely no problem doing what it takes to hit my numbers. I am no stranger to a late night hustle or Saturday morning phone-fest. Business owners do what it takes. Plain and simple.

Knowing that your desk is your own storefront, it is important to define your business. How do you differ from the guy or girl next to you? How do your results differ? Is there anything you can "borrow" from the way they run their business that can help you run yours more smoothly?

I am all about work/life balance. Too many times over the years, I rode that downward spiral of work-work-work/life balance. What's crazy is without disengaging from time to time and taking a break, you actually end up having to work more for the same results.

As a business owner, you have the freedom to take a minute off. When you think of yourself as an employee, you are beholden to your boss. You work in sales. When you don't work it means less income for your employer. Are they really incentivized to tell you to take time off?

You know what is good for "YOU INC." better than anyone else. Do you need to play catch up? Take a few evening or weekend at bats. Need to shut your brain off? Have a "me" day. Just don't make personal days too much of a habit or excuse. It's easy to fall into the "I deserve this" trap while your production slides and you start to deserve it less.

Remember, think and act as if you owned the business. It is amazing what this little shift can do for you.

# KEEP CALM & GET HEALTHY

Relax. It sounded easy enough when Frankie said it, but the fact of the matter is when you are in a sales job, getting proper rest can be damn near impossible.

Getting proper rest is infinitely important when you are a sales professional. I'm not saying you should be taking a siesta every day, but I am telling you that as salespeople, we neglect rest and sleep, often wearing that sleeplessness like a badge of honor.

It's an endless cycle. We aren't sleeping because we are stressed about hitting numbers. We're tossing and turning trying to figure out how we are going to get back on track and salvage our month. We tell ourselves we've got this, but in reality, we are mentally checking off days in the calendar and doing the math. This is going to be a photo-finish.

The lack of sleep doesn't really bother us on day one. We go about our day as usual. We may have a little extra coffee. No big deal. We got this.

That night, the stress and extra caffeine wakes us up in the middle of the night. One day down, X days to go. We do the math. How will we hit quota? What do we need each day? Is there any breathing room, or is each daily goal make or break?

Day two might be just slightly harder. We are dragging just a little bit more. That coffee is going down even easier. Each prospect we talk to means progressively more and more as the clock ticks, and the caffeine has us a little on edge.

On this night, we fall asleep instantly as our body is drained and we tossed back a couple of cocktails to take the edge off.

We wake up a few hours into the night as our stomach begins to digest the alcohol and we start our mental inventory. What did we do today? How many days left to do how much business? Is that client we got a little snarky with going to tattle on us? Should we start working on our resume?

Lather.

Rinse.

Repeat.

As each day goes by, we get a little less sleep and a little more stressed out. We are piling solutions on top of self-inflicted wounds that could be avoided up front.

This is a recipe for disaster. I know it. I have lived it.

I am not a doctor, nor do I play one on television. But I do have Google, and here is what I learned happens to your body and brain when you sleep too little, stress too much, drink too much caffeine and too much alcohol.

-Dehydration

When you are dehydrated, your body depletes itself of sodium and electrolytes, which affect cognitive abilities. It is not unheard of to see a perfectly healthy runner complete a marathon then immediately need medical attention due to being confused and disoriented.

-Lack of sleep

When you don't get enough sleep there are several consequences.

Focus, alertness, concentration, logical thought, memory, and problem solving are all negatively affected when you do not get enough sleep.

When you do not get enough sleep, depression is more likely to set in. Sleeplessness and depression cause a never-ending cycle that is tough to snap out of.

When you don't get enough sleep, chemicals in your brain are triggered that make you feel hungry more often. Not only do you feel hungrier, you crave unhealthy food. Eating this food then can make you less energetic and more lethargic.

-Alcohol

Using alcohol to wind down after a stressful day is common. Here is what happens when it goes to the extreme.

First, the alcohol dehydrates you even more (see above). This is complicated when you wake up hungover and your brain is a dry sponge.

Second, when your body is breaking down the alcohol in the middle of the night, it can wake you up, further complicating things with more lack of sleep, depression, etc…

Next, that hangover can cause you to be a grouch the next day. How can you expect to sell successfully when you can't even think straight?

-Caffeine

So you can't think straight because of your hangover? Pop a Red

Bull Bro!

Think again. That Red Bull is full of sodium along with the pile of stimulants it contains. This dehydrates you (again, see above) even further and affects your mood in more of a negative way than you ever imagined.

I am not saying you need to call Dr. Drew and hit Sales Guy Rehab here. What I am saying is that I have certainly been there and pleaded temporary insanity due to all of this self-inflicted crap before.

In the end, taking some time to get off that hamster wheel and going to bed early with a good book (not even a television in the background) for a few nights can work wonders for your pipeline. It's way better than jumping back into the never-ending stress cycle.

# CHANGE ON THE FLY

What would you do tomorrow if you showed up to work and were told, "We no longer sell appliances. Starting today, we sell cleaning products. Here's your product and pricing sheet, have at it." A small minority of us would be checking LinkedIn within minutes.

Those reading this are a little special however, and are more committed to their craft than some of their counterparts (how else can you explain making it through two and a half books by yours truly so far?). I'll lay the same odds that the majority of my readers will shrug and ask, "Are we selling to commercial or residential?" and start plotting our attack on the market.

Great salespeople aren't just selling a product. They are selling themselves. We've talked about personal branding before and this is where the rubber meets the road. How many customers that have a dishwasher you sold them would also be interested in owning the best mop on the market? If you made an impression, that answer is a lot more favorable, because they'd at least be willing to listen to what you had to say.

I am not trying to tell you that selling a top-shelf product one day then selling golf pencils the next is easy. What I am telling you is that the fundamentals don't change.

The best sales professionals know what makes their customers tick. When they don't, they make sure to find out quickly and non-invasively.

They know how to create solutions from the products to problems the prospects have. Sometimes, the prospect is not even aware they have the problem until the solution is apparent.

Their clients know them as humans first. Not a sales guy, not a suit, not a management weenie, just a person. Clients see eye-to-eye and can talk candidly without fearing that "anything they say can and will be used against them". This is worth its weight in gold. When the customer sees you on their own level, trust is way easier to come by.

Showing that you genuinely care is tantamount to being invited in for a drink. There is an immediate familiarity. You are entering the good version of the friend zone.

It is important to remember that you must remain on equal footing. If you are opening up quite a bit to them, you need to get them to open up to you as well. Otherwise, you are treating them like your shrink, and we ultimately have to be moving toward helping them. Keep in mind that people love talking about themselves (and we do too), so if you find yourself talking too much about your favorite Napa Valley winery, pivot back to them.

Build relationships like this with your prospects and clients and you could be selling rubber bands and still have a client base.

Get to know them, get to understand them, get them to understand you, and you are on your way!

# EVERYBODY HURTS...SOMETIMES

We must go into every sales meeting with a positive mindset. We walk in that room assuming the sale. We are winners!

Why even let failure enter your mind. You are going to be victorious. Thinking anything else is just admitting weakness. Why would you assume failure? You are a sales machine!!!

Wait. What's that you say? We only actually close less than fifty percent of the clients we pitch to at that first meeting? Maybe it's time to rethink that "All I do is win, win, win, no mattah what." mentality. You need an exit strategy.

How sweet was it in that one movie from the eighties when the cool guy goes up to the girl and gets shot down instantly and he walks away with a too cool for school "Well fuck you then."

That was funny, but what are the odds of him having a second shot? Perhaps more importantly, what are the chances that her friends heard him say that or will hear about it later. Then, what are the chances they tell their friends and now his reputation is cemented.

Back to our sales meeting, you should absolutely walk in there assuming that you will make the sale. Assumptive attitude, assumptive posture, assumptive phrasing, the whole nine yards. But be prepared for a no.

When you are preparing for your meeting, you should already be prepping to handle their questions and objections as they come in. How much harder is it really to have a pre-planned exit strategy for when those objections become all too real and the speed bumps turn into roadblocks?

Unlike the cool guy in the movie, we need to handle this with grace. But how do we do this?

First, like the sign says, KEEP CALM. We came in knowing there was a chance this might happen, so we shouldn't be surprised or be ready to burn a bridge.

Second, thank them. "Thank you for sharing your concerns Jon. I never want a client to jump in before they've done their homework and are comfortable with the decision to move forward with me." With this, we are still assuming the sale, just not this minute.

Next, put the blame firmly on your own shoulders. "Before I go, let me recap your questions and concerns please. It is plain to me that I missed something when we originally spoke because I didn't address this. I apologize and will research your concerns further." It is important that we shoulder the burden here. No matter how you feel at the time, this is not where you blame them for not paying attention or leading you on.

Our next step is to set a solid follow-up appointment. This is not only firm on a time and date, but expectations should be properly set. "Ok Jon, I have us penciled in for next Wednesday the 14th at 2pm. I will be sure to have the answers you seek. I will make sure I get as much of the paperwork done up front as possible to make things easier for you. If you need to reschedule, please let me know ahead of time, Are we still looking at a one month delivery window?" Here, we are not only letting them know we expect to get ink on the contract next time, but giving them one last chance to object if they are still just being polite. If they are just kicking tires, more than likely they will tell us NOT to have that paperwork pre-filled out because they will feel guilty for letting you do so.

As a recap, you should 100% always go in with a winning mindset. If you don't go in with your parachute loaded, you will be kissing 100% of the noes permanently goodbye without a chance of converting them to a yes at a later date.

It might seem cool to be that eighties movie character, but that guy probably still lives with his mom.

# PATTERNUS INTERRUPTUS

The average salesperson's conversation is 80/20. They talk 80 percent and the prospect talks 20 percent. Not only is this average, this is the norm.

This is why people smell a salesman from a mile away and run in the other direction with a bubble saying "I'm just looking..." hanging in the air where they once stood.

Why is this?

If they are looking for a particular product, and we offer said product, why do they treat us like we are trying to eat their brains?

For starters, it's your approach.

Are you approaching them in a friendly, non-threatening manner, or are you saying "how can I help you? Or, Is there anything I can help you find?". Even though you are being friendly, asking them a yes or no question leaves you nowhere to maneuver to. Asking them the same question they are expecting to hear and have a ready-answer for gets you nowhere even faster.

Toss in a little pattern interrupting question to disrupt their synapses. Get them thinking.

If I worked at say, a department store, I might approach them and ask what the next three events they have to dress for are. If I worked at Foot Locker, I'd ask how many months there gym shoes tend to last. Selling TVs? Ask how many hours a week the set will be used. These are all relevant questions, but they will all force a little bit of thought.

I have a tricky one I use in my field. I ask everyone how long they plan on owning the home. Eighty percent of the time, they think I am asking so I can steer them into a short-term adjustable loan and they hit me with "I only want a fixed rate". Then I flip the script. "Absolutely, I actually was asking that question so we can see what fixed term suits you best. You see...". From there I go into more of a financial advisor role and question their ideas on finance right alongside them.

Once you jar them out of zombie shopper mode with some well placed disruptors, it is easier to ask relevant questions that get the conversation going in the right direction. When you feel the conversation starting to get a little dry, disrupt them again.

Some questions to ask:

"So what do you do for fun?"

"Are you fully funding your retirement accounts?"

"Are your kids on a scholarship track?"

"Do you play video games?"

"Do you have Netflix?"

"How much do you love Amazon Prime?"

"Are you a talk radio guy?"

"You play sports?"

"You a sports fan?"

"Raisin Bran or Corn Flakes?"

"Mac or PC?"

"Iphone or Android?"

Many of these questions will sometimes get "Why do you need to know?" tossed back at you, if they are tentative, so have a response ready "It tells me a lot about who you are. We actually have apps for iOS and Android, but they are a little different in their approach." "If you are fully funding your 401k, I have different approaches to your mortgage than if you weren't".

The key is follow-up questions. No matter what their answer is, have something to hit them with until you get them talking about themselves. When you get them there, you are leaving "the sales guy" zone and entering "the friend zone". Unlike your college crush though, this is a friend zone you want to be in.

# NO MOBY DICKS

You've been there before. During your initial triage, you find out a prospect has been shopping around in your industry for years, but never pulled the trigger.

Further, they have actually gotten close to the finish line with one or more of your competitors only to pull out for one reason or another.

They've never met you before though. You're different. You not only offer a superior product, but you yourself are part of the overall package. This time will be different.

You see them as a challenge. You put on your Sunday best and wine them, dine them, you are unstoppable and they are eating it up.

As you finish your day, you have an internal chuckle at the suckers who couldn't close these folks in the past. They couldn't hold a candle to you. You are the salesman's salesman. A man among boys.

Don't count those chickens just yet, Mr. Gekko. That client you just wined and dined? They are more addicted to the thrill of being wooed by you than any high your product can give them. You just bought yourself a one way ticket to headache-land. And we're out of Tylenol.

You better get them signed, sealed and delivered with quickness, because as soon as your reality distortion field wears off and they are left to their own world, a Google search bar, and their own spreadsheets, you'll be out in the cold with the other schmoes in no time.

You've seen it play out. Suddenly, the price is too high, they found a complaint about you online, their barber says they need a 15th opinion, they prayed on it, they're too busy at work, etc...They love the attention, but fear commitment.

In the mortgage business, I see these every single day.

We have government products that offer folks a serious life preserver. Even if you aren't in a bind, these programs allow for dead simple approval with solid pricing and benefits. These amazing products have been around for seven and a half years, and we've been threatened by the powers that be that they will go away forever quite soon.

At one point, a solid majority of homeowners in the US qualified for these programs and thankfully, most have taken advantage. I find about 2 or 3 a week that actually fully qualify on all fronts but cannot answer the question of why they haven't taken advantage of it yet.

That's right. Ninety months of overpaying for their home loan that could have been improved at no risk to them at any time during that span.

I do pretty well with these folks. Some will never be converted because they subconsciously believe they don't deserve it. Some will never be converted because they don't trust anyone but themselves. Some don't do it because they think they missed the "gold rush" and don't want to settle.

Some actually listen to the facts though and when I present to them the savings they missed out on over 90 months, it serves as a big enough slap to get them motivated.

My point here is this. When you chase after the white whales of the world, you will get a rush. They will also get that same rush because you are a new salesperson at their beck and call. You must keep them in the honeymoon phase as long as you can, because the second you stop the dog and pony, they start to doubt you, themselves, the product and the company.

Yes, there are exceptions. Sometimes, you get a whale that's tired of swimming and realizes it's just time to buy already. You might even luck out and get a referral sent to you by friends, family or a past client that just needs someone they can really trust.

More often than not though, you will expend a lot of energy getting Moby Dick in the door to start the process, countless hours keeping them on board during the process and even more energy to get them to finally close the deal. This one client can cost you five or six other clients if you are not careful and get obsessed.

# START SMART

If it is important to get off to a hot start so we get out of the gates strong, what can we do to ensure this happens?

We've talked about recapping our day. How about starting our daily plan for tomorrow tonight?

It's simple. When you are doing your daily recap, think about a few easy ones.

1.  What metrics goals did we hit today? If we hit them, what did we do to make that happen? If we didn't, what did we do (or not do) that caused us to miss?

2.  Did we hit our production goal? If so, what did we do to get there? If not, why?

3.  What is your carryover hot-list for tomorrow? These are your hot prospects that just need a little massaging to get on board. Every night, you should be carrying over a few leads that you know will be your next sales.

4.  Who are your warm follow-ups for tomorrow? These are the carryover hot-list clients of the future and must be worked accordingly.

5.  Who are we calling, emailing or mailing a "thank you" to tomorrow? These should include closed clients and the ones that got away. You'll be amazed at the amount of referrals I have

received from folks who didn't do business with me but liked me nonetheless.

6.     Study your calendar and adjust it accordingly. Make sure appointments are in a logical order at logical times.

This list can go on and on and on, but you get the picture. I cheat and use a notebook with separate boxes so I can keep this very organized.

This is key though. Ever jump on a treadmill going full speed? You are sure to fall on your face. The same thing happens when you get to the office at 8:59 am unprepared.

This little exercise lets you know ahead of time what you are getting into. I give myself a quick refresher in the morning on my phone before I leave the house and I hit the road. Whether I get to my desk at 8:30 am or 9:01 am, I am prepared for what my day brings. I attack the day. It does not attack me.

# SHOW THEM YOU CARE

Your customers are coming to you for a reason. They are looking for a solution to a problem. This is the same whether you sell televisions, insurance, mortgages, windows, clothing, software, snow removal, the list goes on.

People run away from pain and toward pleasure, right? Common sense would say we need to swoop in and save the day the very moment we realize we can solve their particular problem. And this would be wrong.

Sales are made on emotion and justified with logic. The common sense is secondary.

Recognizing we can solve their problem is great. Now hold that card close to the vest.

We need to apply the 80/20 rule here. Let them tell you their problem. Ask them more questions. Go deep on it. How does it make them feel? What other issues arise as a result? Does it affect their bottom line? Does it cause added stress? More work? Consume more time?

Let them rat hole themselves. They have been here before, which is exactly why we are speaking to them right now. Get them as worked up about their particular problem. Let them come clean about everything they are holding inside.

Then let them know you can help. This is the way to win their hearts and minds, instead of just their minds.

Think about the emotions involved in your sales presentation.

If they give us their problem and we solve it in the first five minutes of the meeting, we are not only minimizing the value of our product, but we also reduce ourselves to order taking.

Not a bad way to earn a living, but think about it from the prospect's perspective. If we can solve their problem so easily, I bet the next guy can too. There is nothing stopping them from grabbing the yellow pages and shopping based solely on price. Now we are forced to negotiate against every other cut rate yahoo in the book.

The client is down in the dumps for about 3% of the meeting because we rode in on our white horse and saved the day. You'd think they'd be beholden to us, but they aren't, because we haven't connected with them on a personal and emotional level.

Now let's look at it the way I described a few paragraphs up.

We let them vent. Really vent. Treat it like an onion. Every layer we peel away stinks a little more and gets them closer to tears. Ask questions. How do they feel when this problem arises? What are the secondary and tertiary effects, etc…

If we do this right, we have them really craving a solution to their issue. This is where we let them know "I've got just the thing to solve your problem".

At this point, they are emotionally invested in the meeting and you. You have shown that you care about them. You aren't here just to fix the water heater, you are hear to listen to them vent about the cold shower and how they couldn't take it so they had to shower at the gym and walk on the gross locker room floor and were late to work because their routine was thrown off.

You are a human helping another human. You are not a robot ticking off another metric. This client will not shop you. You both won.

Now, I want to make a bold assumption here that you actually have a heart and do genuinely care about your clients. If you do, this should come easy to you. If you don't, you may need to make an appointment with the Wizard Tin Man because you really should give a shit about your customers.

I mention this part because they are still those detractors out there who want to characterize sales professionals as sleazy and manipulative. These folks would say we are manipulating our clients when we push their buttons.

Do I think having the approach above is manipulative? No. I think we are truly getting to the root of a problem so we can properly solve it. If you truly do care about helping people, this will come easily to you.

# BE PLEASURABLE

The phone rings. You don't recognize the number, but you answer anyway.

The call starts...

"Congratulations! You just won a free cruise!"

Or

"We are calling from your credit card account."

It's a constant game of whack-a-mole. We train ourselves to recognize the numbers, and they change their numbers. It's maddening. We hate telemarketers!

These folks are definitely the extreme end of the spectrum, but the fact of the matter is that we are raised to dislike salespeople.

Why though? Don't they offer a valid service?

The majority of the time, we dislike salespeople because we don't want to be pushed into a decision. As humans, we like to do things on our own terms. It is uncomfortable to us when someone pushes that timetable.

Here's the truth. In a successful sales transaction, there should ALWAYS be a moment where everyone is uncomfortable.

The customer should have butterflies because they are about to make a decision that changes their life in some way.

We should have that uneasy feeling because we are asking them to do so.

The crazy part is that lurking just beyond those butterflies is happiness and tranquility with a side of accomplishment. Once they say yes, all is right in the world for both of you. Everybody wins.

Yet, it is just this uneasy feeling that has us dancing around the sale and them avoiding us.

We must show them that the feelings that follow the consummation of the sale will far outweigh the pain they feel on the road to getting there.

# SHOW THEM YOU UNDERSTAND

In our respective fields, when we go about our day to day, it is very easy to fall into a "Who's next?" mentality. We go through our days, weeks, and months moving from client to client, and on a macro scale, they all start to look, feel, and sound the same.

This can cause countless issues as we over generalize and prejudge our prospects, assuming we know what's best for them before we actually do triage and diagnose.

Would you want a doctor who came in, asked you what was wrong, then left the room, only to return 3 minutes later with a prescription? All without running any sort of tests or doing an exam?

Sadly, this is exactly what we do to our clients much of the time. We assume their problems and goals are the same as the last guy and rush to a conclusion because we start thinking that is what they want.

One of the biggest complaints in client facing business these days is that the customer doesn't feel like a human. We are treating them like numbers without knowing or meaning to do so.

You wouldn't ask someone out on a date then promptly treat them no better than anyone else would you? If you don't show them how special they are, chances are you won't be getting a second date. People need warm fuzzies.

A surefire way to eradicate the warm and fuzzies is to just treat them like the next prospect in a long line of similar prospects.

When researching a client prior to a meeting, I like to take a few minutes and really try to put myself in their shoes. "Why were they initially attracted to my product?", "Why my product/company/me in particular?", "Why now?", "What's in it for them?".

The last one, WHAT'S IN IT FOR THEM? Or WIIFM (pronounced whiff 'em) for short is really the one to focus on here. We know that our product is a solution to a problem. What will they get as a result of solving said problem?

Putting yourself in their shoes is the easiest way to describe empathy. We must strive to feel what our clients are feeling at all times.

When you are able to show your clients that you understand them and the reason why they are working with you, their WIIFM becomes clearer to both of you and they are able to understand that you indeed "get" them. They know that you have their best interest at heart and they are not just another notch in your belt. When you truly care, it will show through. It is OK to show them that you are human.

# DON'T BE A SALESMAN

I had a guy working for me a few years back. A solid hand as they say. He had a background in pretty much door-to-door sales. As a rookie, he out-shined everyone for his first few months. He was my shining star and I was ecstatic to have him on my team.

After a few months, the other rookies started catching up to him. His confidence wavered some, so I started paying more attention to him. What I found, is that I should have been paying more attention to him from day one, but this is not a sales management book, so enough about me...

I listened to some of his sales calls, and his door-to-door tactics were shining brightly. Some of them a little too brightly. He was presenting to clients like he had to keep a foot in the door the entire time. When you are selling cleaning products, vacuums, magazine subscriptions, or brushes you need to keep your foot in the door and not let them shut you out.

With financial services however, it can include (doesn't have to, but can) a little more bake time. People legit have to speak with spouses, parents, financial planners, etc... If we are setting up our presentation properly, we don't need to keep a foot in that door, because we are given the key to come back whenever we want.

After hearing him building a straw-man argument up with a prospect, I asked him to take a walk. His antennae shot up because this may not have been our first heart-to-heart.

When I sat him down my first statement was "You sound like a salesman".

He thanked me.

Then I said, "I don't want you to."

And he scrunched up his face and couldn't comprehend. He was proud of his days selling stuff door-to-door and prided himself on being a "salesman".

To me, his version of a salesman was a guy in red suspenders and a straw hat barking out that he'd guess your weight.

I do not think he had the wrong intentions. I think he had the wrong impressions.

In his view of sales, there is one winner and one sucker.

In my vision, there is a mutually beneficial transaction.

He and I began working right then and there on some more advanced techniques that I knew he could handle.

The biggest takeaway from our meetings was teaching him not to trap a client.

When someone is backed into a corner, their only option is to fight their way out.

What this guy was doing was either getting the sale early, or backing them into that proverbial corner. His training was to keep churning and burning until that bridge was toast.

He was Lenny from Of Mice and Men. He petted his pet mouse over and over and harder and harder until the mouse was worn out.

My assignment for him was to "corral" his clients. I made a circle with my hands, fingertips touching and made him envision holding his clients in the circle but letting them move freely. I didn't want him to crush the client.

This visual was taken to heart and became our signal any time I heard him (and eventually others) squeezing too tight.

When you give clients an out, it short circuits their "sales guy defense shields". They don't know what to think. "You mean I can escape this conversation without making up some lame excuse about a sick relative?" They leave the sales presentation calm. They leave us without despising us for pushing them too hard. They leave us with the proper expectation of follow-up and action.

That's right, we give them the out. We let them know it's OK that we aren't moving forward right now because we know they aren't ready and we don't want to pressure them. We do, however, let them know that we will follow up in X hours or X days to get the ball rolling. The expectation is set that we will be moving forward once they are comfortable.

The key is, they don't feel trapped. The door is still open on both sides, but they know we will be moving forward at the next meeting.

The hard follow-up is key. If the client was going to smokescreen us with the sick uncle and disappear act, we will never hear back from them. We never would have gained this client anyway.

What we want to focus on is that percentage of our client base that truly was on the fence and would have run for the hills if we squeezed any tighter. We've all had this happen. We pushed just a little too hard and the next guy who coddled them took all of our ideas and sold the client. The client probably even handed him our proposal.

Remember, this chapter is not about becoming soft. It is not free license to become a total wuss. We still need to grab the ripe ones just as we recognize they are ready and capitalize.

All I am saying is that if the average consumer doesn't want to be sold, there is no reason to act like we are selling them. Keep them corralled, don't smother them and you will win. What's great is that they will be winning too.

Quick bonus tip.

People tend to agree with things when you state them as fact.

One of my favorite "pressure moves" is to foreshadow up front that I am not high pressure at all.

"I promise, I am not high pressure. In fact, I often tell people NOT to move forward because it really doesn't make any sense. So you have my word that if I don't have a solution for you, I will tell you so. You also have my word that if something is truly good for you, I WILL apply some pressure, because you just might need that little push to get you started."

Now, I just told you that I will ONLY pressure you if something really makes sense. I have told you this during our fact-finding interview and haven't even shown you a product at all.

When I do show you your options, subconsciously, you will only expect me to give you any pressure IF something is good for you. You also didn't object when I told you I would do this early on.

We have an understanding. You cannot be mad at me for closing multiple times because we have uncovered the product for you!

# YOU JUST GOT A RAISE

Let's get this out of the way right here and now. The clock is always ticking. As a matter of fact, I am writing this chapter on the 2nd of the month and I am already thinking about my monthly goal.

Time truly is the great equalizer. We all have the same amount of minutes in our day, so why is it that some of us are always seemingly blasting through the end of the month like Kramer from Seinfeld busting in the door while others are sitting back on the 25th, stress-free?

Part of it has to do with personality and character. Some of us need that added pressure of a deadline to get things done while others cannot operate without being ahead of the curve.

Most of the time however, this comes down to time management.

Parkinson's Law states "work expands so as to fill the time available for its completion". Ever wonder why we tend to cram for tests last minute or crap out a term paper the night before it's due? You can thank our man Cyril Northcote Parkinson. You are, after all, just abiding by the law!

Let's think about how we can get ahead of the curve here.

Let's look at the macro. Do you find yourself stressing and struggling to hit your goal by month end? You are not alone, my friend. Yours truly has spent many a 29th burning the midnight oil. I have learned my lessons though. When you are under the gun, you are not on your A game. Hell, you are probably at about your P game, because this is when you start to be a little bit pushy and pressure your clients to move forward before they are ready.

The easiest way I see to remedy this is proper goal setting. We delve more deeply into this in Sell Smarter (book 1 of this series), but in a nutshell, why not break your goals down into more manageable chunks? For instance, I like to set my weekly goal at 30% of my monthly quota. This way, I know that as long as I hit 2 or 3 of those weeklies, I am 75-90% to my monthly goal going into the final week. Less pressure ON ME means I am exerting less pressure on my customers. Everybody wins!

Let's break it down even further. What do we need to do each day to hit that weekly figure? How many calls, appointments, applications, etc… does it take each day to hit that number? These need to become "must hits" each day in order to succeed.

Here's where it gets more fun. At the end of the day, write down everything you accomplished or spent time on. Take an honest inventory of everything you did that day and ask yourself a binary question. "Can I honestly say that this time was spent in a way that moved me closer to my next sale?"

You will be amazed how much time you spend either treading water or sometimes moving backwards.

What can you trim out of your day tomorrow? How can you reconfigure your schedule so you are ahead of the game before lunch? It's much easier to hit the field at halftime with a lead isn't it?

I don't want you to cancel sales meetings, team huddles, or

sessions with coaches or mentors. I want you to cut out the 3 laps you do of the office kibbitzing with your co-workers. I want you to cut out smoke breaks. If you are on the road, I want you to schedule appointments in a way that you can hit them one after the other geographically rather than add drive time for drive time's sake. Spend time on business, not just busy-ness.

By doing this exercise, let's just say you cut out the minimum of 30 minutes per day of calendar bloat. That's an average of an extra 10 hours per business month. How much easier is it to hit that goal when you have an entire extra day to do it? Find an hour a day to re-purpose and you have nearly THREE business days added to your month.

Congratulations, you just gave yourself a raise.

# HONE YOUR SCHTICK

It's a fact that people want to buy from people they like. We've established this over and over.

Think about your last good sales call. How was the rapport? If the call was good, you know they liked you. How did you get them to like you though?

What better way to get them to like you than to make them laugh? Not only does this help break down that defensive moat our customers sometimes start with, but it gets them smiling. When they smile, their brain releases dopamine, endorphins and serotonin, which instantly lowers their guard (and their blood pressure).

A great side effect of their laughter is that smiles are contagious. You'll be smiling along with them and your confidence will receive a boost, knowing that you are winning them over.

I have found that the absolute easiest way to get a chuckle is to toss in a little self-deprecating humor. This is a very safe way to get them going and also lets the customer know that you don't take yourself that seriously. This also serves to humanize you.

If you've cleared it first, throwing out a couple of witty barbs about your boss works too. Who can't relate to having a boss? They get to live vicariously through you while you needle them. "My boss is probably going to have a fit when he sees this pricing

I gave you, but better him than us, right?"

There are, however, a few key elements you need to keep in mind when injecting humor into a sales presentation.

Think more Seinfeld and less Andrew "Dice" Clay. Even if a client takes a conversation below the belt, it is important that we remember why we are there, what are role is, and how we should represent.

**Never make the competition the butt of your joke.**

It has been said before, but when it comes to the competition, always take the high road. I'm of the mindset that whether they are ahead of me or behind me, if I knock the competition down two pegs, the very act of doing so knocks me down those same two pegs so you don't gain any ground. Instead, create separation by building yourself up and emphasizing a feature or benefit you know your competition cannot offer. You'll get ahead without compromising integrity.

**When in doubt, leave it out.**

We don't know our clients outside of our working relationship, so leave stereotypes, racial, political and religious humor to the professionals. All it takes is a slip of the tongue to see a good conversation go bad. A bad conversation leads to an alienated client and could result in unemployment for you.

**Rehearse!**

Think you have a great one-liner that can't miss? Run it by a co-worker for approval. Stumble across a great line that kills on a sales call? Write it down and practice it. Remember, every new prospect is a fresh audience. Hone that material and use it over and over and over until you are sick of saying it. If it works, it works.

# READ MORE BOOKS!

If you are reading this book, you are on the right track. As a sales professional, you need to read.

You should be constantly reading. At any given time, you should be working your way through one book for pleasure and one professional book.

I used to be a book completist. I wouldn't allow myself to start reading a new book until I finished one. I am not sure where I got this trait, but it may be related to why I always compartmentalize my meals as well. I finish my fries before my burger or my burger before my fries. I rarely eat them simultaneously.

One day it hit me that if I could keep track of sports or the plots of different television shows, I was smart enough to read multiple books at the same time. Along these lines, I learned to take a break from a book that wasn't doing it for me rather than trudge through it.

It should be plainly obvious while I want you to read books relating to your profession, I want you te work toward being more well- rounded as well. It is important that we are constantly looking to better ourselves. If you are not growing, you're dying and keeping the knowledge spigot open is a surefire way to keep growing.

As you continue to read more and more in your field, you will start to realize that many of the books you read will have the same messages. This is normal. The more an idea, tactic, or tip is reinforced, the more confidence you will have that it is true. The tips, tricks and tactics I share in my books are not rocket science and not unique. I merely have my own way of packaging and sharing them that you hopefully enjoy more than reading a boring textbook.

As you grow in your field, you will sometimes even wonder if the author is stealing your ideas. This is also perfectly normal. Just like we have covered elsewhere, you are rarely reinventing wheels in sales. Tried and true methods have been tested over time. Sometimes we pick up on them without even realizing it. Sometimes, we just naturally do the right things.

A time may come where you say "I know enough to write one of these books". It happened to me. I actually encourage you to do so. I think I can learn something from everybody, so I'd love to read your book and learn a bit from you!

So if amassing knowledge in our field will help us earn more money, why waste time with trivialities like reading for pleasure?

Firstly, we need an escape. All work and no play as they say. It's OK to veg out in front of the old boob tube from time to time or spend a night at the movies. We need to get away from work sometimes. Reading a great book gives you that escape in a way that being force fed audio-visual stimuli just can't. Reading sparks your imagination and engages parts of your brain that TV or movies just don't hit.

When you read for fun, you are also learning new things. Your vocabulary grows. You subconsciously engage the problem solving parts of your brain when there is a conflict. You become a better salesperson.

For me, there is an added benefit. As someone who sells almost exclusively by phone, I don't have the luxury of meeting my clients face-to-face. It is important at the same time to build a picture of what they look like and who they are outside of the disembodied voice we get to know them as.

Ever read a book, then see the movie and think that you didn't picture a character looking or acting like the actor who portrayed them? I have had this happen with clients countless times. I meet them or they send me a picture of them in their new home and I see the real person. It can be jarring sometimes.

Along those same lines, have you ever seen a preview for a movie for a book or seen the entire movie itself before you read the book? To me, this kills some of the magic of the book because my imagination is given a shortcut. It's as if I cheated.

Trust me when I tell you that your professional life will be enriched when you choose to start reading for pleasure.

The great part about this is that there are literally MILLIONS of books out there to choose from. I don't care what you read, I just care that you read. I promise that no matter what you choose, it will help you in the end. Your brain will be sharper as a result.

When it comes to professional books, you are already reading one, so you are on the right track. When you finish this one, I know two other solid offerings by a very handsome author you can check out.

If you need suggestions, I am happy to assist. Drop me a line at scott@30minutesalescoach.com and I will be happy to offer up some ideas. I am constantly working my way through books in various genres, so I know I can find something to get you on track.

# THANK YOU

Thank you.

Always thank your prospects and customers. No matter how the transaction or conversation goes, it costs you nothing to thank them and it smooths over many a rough spots.

With that being said, it is time for me to give each and every one of you out there a firm virtual handshake and let you know how grateful I am that you took the time to read my book (or books). With so many options out there vying for your eyeballs, it means a ton to me that I got the nod.

I said it in the first few paragraphs of this book that I really did write these three books for you.

There were some ulterior motives though.

First, I needed to get some of this alphabet soup of ideas out of my head and onto paper before they biodegraded.

Second, I had a strong desire to prove to myself that I actually could write a book. The idea seemed so mountainous that I was scared to take that first step and procrastinated it for years.

Writing three shorter form books allowed me to prove to myself that I could do it. When you add them all up, the 30 Minute Sales Coach "trilogy" is a pretty nice sized pile of paper.

For now, I am done writing sales books. It is time for me to pursue the next challenge of writing fiction. I am not going anywhere though. The podcast is still going strong, and you can reach out to me anytime you need a helping hand.

Thank you again.

# FROM THE AUTHOR

With so many options available to you, I am grateful you chose to read this book.

When I set out to start The 30 Minute Sales Coach series, I had a very rough idea of where I was headed with it, but my road map was back-of-a-napkin to say the least. I knew I wanted to help people. I knew I had something to share. I had no idea just how many people would choose to purchase and read my first book.

The early success of Sell Smarter told me I was on to something. People were not only choosing to read my book, but they were finding takeaways that they could easily implement in their game and succeeding. In my heart, I knew there was good info there, but my methods are a little unorthodox, to say the least, and require you to not take yourself all that seriously.

Between the overwhelming response from readers about Sell Smarter, and the feedback from listeners of The Seven Minute Sales Minute, it is clear that there is a niche to be filled. Clear and concise sales advice that is free of trite lingo is the aim here. My goal is to be able to show you how to sell in a way that is not only mutually beneficial for you and your customer, but also in a manner that allows you to sleep at night. I want to show you that you don't need to be a sales-bully or resort to trickery to do your job.

There <u>can</u> be integrity in sales.

With this endpoint in mind, I knew this series had to continue and Sell Even Smarter was a book that needed to be written.

I know who and what I am and make no false claims. I'm no rocket scientist. I'm no motivational speaker. I am not an internet-lifestyle guru. I am a salesman. I am good at what I do and I know how to break it down for you. My analogies and stories may be slightly sophomoric at times. I'm not writing textbooks here though.

Take each chapter as a separate lesson and enjoy the homework. It's designed to be engaging and entertaining. Most of all have fun.

Please take a moment and review this book when you are done reading. (www.30MinuteSalesCoach.com)

Additionally, if there are any topics you would like to see tackled in the next book, feel free to email me. I would love to hear from you! - scott@30minutesalescoach.com


Thank you,
Scott Fishman

# ABOUT THE AUTHOR

Husband and father first, Scott lives in Bloomfield Hills, Michigan with his amazingly supportive wife, Beth and his two dogs, Louis and Coco.

To this day, Scott is still active in his sales career at one of the country's largest mortgage lenders. After nearly two decades in that industry, he is convinced he will be doing it forever. Over the years, he has been able to lead, coach, grow and mentor an entire generation of salespeople.

In his spare time, Scott and his pal Jon co-host **The Seven Minute Sales Minute** podcast which has a rapidly growing audience.

www.ingramcontent.com/pod-product-compliance
Lightning Source LLC
Chambersburg PA
CBHW030940180526
45163CB00002B/648